What International Managers and *th - M*
Say Abou

...a blend of wit and wisdom to stimulat   to be
saved up for the plane; read it well befo

                                             ~..~~ International, UK

Markets are becoming more global, and our management are being called on more and more to think and act within an international context.

    This book is full of excellent suggestions on how to be more sensitive to the values and cultures of others and how to communicate better in the global marketplace.

                Dr Martin Posth
                Member of the Board of Management
                Volkswagen AG, Germany

...for everyone who has to do business with people from other countries...stimulates the reader to study and understand how much a different cultural background influences our speech and behavior...I really enjoyed reading this book.

                Gunnar Lennerheim
                Corporate Human Resources and
                Organization, Ericsson, Sweden

...those tips and snippets of information which the conscientious manager holds about other cultures have now become the new stereotypes, and must be reviewed... This book is never boring, and encourages participation through questions and exercises with answers which sometimes surprise.

                Richard Brown
                Human Relations Directorate
                Airbus Industrie, France

If a Japanese rep is failing to sell an Italian car to a Finn in the US, he should read *The International Business Book*. He might not sell the car, but at least he'll understand why...

                Jean Sembertrand
                Communication Manager
                Sandoz Pharma, Switzerland

This book is both informative and instructive for creative global managers in international communications.
                Toshio Baba
                Chairman and CEO
                Tokyo Consulting Boutique Inc, Japan

For the manager involved in international business, it's an accessible and entertaining read.
                Sarah Hegarty
                Management Week

Approachably written and mercifully short...hugely worth the effort for anyone engaged in international business.

                Francis Kinsman
                Management Today

The International Business *Book*

Vincent Guy   John Mattock

Printed on recyclable paper

NTC Business Books

a division of *NTC Publishing Group* • Lincolnwood, Illinois USA

Library of Congress Cataloging-in-Publication Data
Guy, Vincent.
  The international business book: all the tools, tactics, and tips
you need for doing business across cultures/Vincent Guy,
John Mattock.
    p.   cm.
  Includes bibliographical references and index.
  ISBN 0-8442-3517-2
  1. International business enterprises—Management. I. Mattock,
John. II. Title.
  HD62.4.G89 1995
  658' .049—dc20   94-16173
                                                               CIP

Published in the United States in 1995 by NTC Business Books,
a division of NTC Publishing Group, 4255 West Touhy Avenue,
Lincolnwood (Chicago), Illinois 60646-1975, U.S.A.
©1993, 1991 by Canning. All rights reserved.
No part of this book may be reproduced, stored
in a retrieval system, or transmitted in any form or by any means,
electronic, mechanical, photocopying, recording or otherwise, without
the prior permission of NTC Publishing Group.
This edition first published in the United Kingdom in 1991 by Kogan Page,
120 Pentonville Road, London N1 9JN.
Manufactured in the United States of America.

4 5 6 7 8 9 0 VP 9 8 7 6 5 4 3 2 1

Contents

▲6 Talk

Acknowledgments

We wish to thank all those friends, colleagues and clients who have encouraged us and fed us with ideas.

We are grateful to staff and course members at the Centre for International Briefing, Farnham Castle, and particularly Jehad Al Omari and Joseph Mutaboba.

The text or parts of it were read by Ben Ball, John Ferguson, Ian Fleming, Russell Harlow, Susanna Lyddon, Sandy Macdonald, Tina Moskal, Frank Riess, Eleni Scondra, David Wilson Ward and Peter Wright. Thanks to them for their comments, almost all of which we have acted upon.

The quiz in Chapter 4 (Golden Rules) was developed and the results collated by Robin Little, to whom we give our thanks.

Tony Buzan's ideas in *Use Your Head* (1974, BBC) were adapted for use in Chapter 5 (the concentration span exercise), and we gratefully acknowledge that source.

We are grateful to the following for permission to quote extracts: Basil Blackwell (*Strategies and Styles,* by Michael Goold and Andrew Campbell); Harper Collins (*Churchill's Black Dog,* by Anthony Storr); William Heinemann Ltd. (*Behind the Wall,* by Colin Thubron); *The Independent* (Ties of Anglo-German Friendship, Editorial, March 31, 1990); Martin Secker & Warburg Ltd. (*France in the 1980s,* by John Ardagh); John Wiley & Sons Ltd. (*Beyond Negotiation,* by John A. Carlisle and Robert C. Parker, 1989). Every effort was made to trace the copyright holders of "The Man Who Never Was", by Ewen Montague, which we read in a 1968 Corgi reprint.

Tina Moskal did the illustrations, and also helped greatly with suggestions for editing. Thanks also to Patrick Frean, who drew the pyramid.

In the course of the book, there are numerous generalizations. We have tried very hard to make sure they are not expressions of prejudice, and apologize in advance to any individual who feels affronted. The opinions expressed and any mistakes of fact are entirely ours.

Vincent Guy
John Mattock

Introduction

This book is for you if you are involved in any kind of international business. You might be a marketing executive with a telecommunications group, an export salesperson in machine tools, a progress chaser in civil engineering or a human resources manager in an insurance company—in fact, you might be anybody who works with people from other countries.

In our seminars at Canning we advise businesspeople on how to communicate. They come from many countries and from diverse fields. They work for large corporations, middle-sized niche companies and small consultancy firms. This book draws both on our experience and theirs.

We hope the book will stimulate you to think and act in new ways when you are doing international business. Our particular interest is in how you deal with people face to face—how you communicate.

To give shape to our ideas, we started from the most basic model of antagonism

and decided it was exactly what we did *not* want. So we thought about where it might lead:

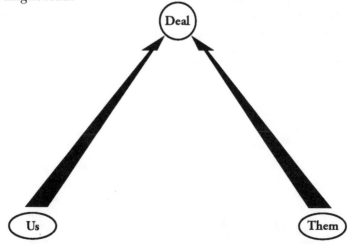

and then broke the process down into a series of steps up the pyramid:

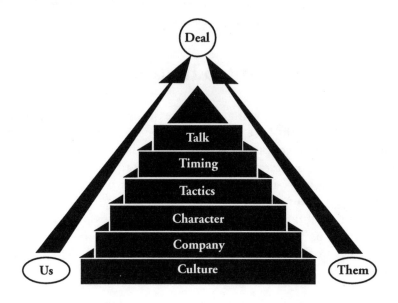

which gave us the chapter headings for the book.

The first three are the constants: whatever deal you are hoping to strike, it will be influenced by the background culture, company style and individual character of your partner.

You will need to think deeply about these constants before moving on to the more transient matters further up the pyramid. The more homework you have done on the constants, the more effectively you can make decisions about your tactics, the timing of activities and the way the talking (and listening) should be done.

This book can be read and worked with during a flight or train journey. You will need a pencil to do the quizzes and exercises.

CHAPTER ONE

Culture

Your business partners' background culture—
the way of life they were raised in—will affect
their approach to every decision.

There are no foreign lands; only the traveller is foreign.

R.L. Stevenson

The World

Communication is a growth business; the world has been shrinking for quite some time. In 1750 it took 12 days to get a message from New York to Boston; a century later, it took 12 hours. Today in 12 hours you can fly from London to Tokyo, and you can send a fax to the other side of the world in 12 seconds. Satellites merge the world's media. Teleconferencing systems link executives across long distances without even the buffer-time of a plane journey. Computer screen trading enables the banker to deal at the touch of a button, shifting currencies and shares at the speed of light.

Does all this mean the end of the personal touch? Will the businessperson in the twenty-first century sit isolated in a bunker, finger on the button? In some areas the answer must be yes: wherever business revolves on commodity-style, single-issue transactions (I buy/You sell/What price?) automation will increase, requiring only a 22-year-old with hot reflexes to pilot the hardware, no matter how many millions are at risk.

But there are other transactions growing in importance and within international reach. Apart from the traditional exporting of tangible goods, deals like the following are mushrooming.

Takeovers and mergers to acquire know-how

- Swiss pharmaceutical company absorbs gene-splicers in the United States

- BASF sets up joint plastics lab in Tokyo, with eight Japanese firms, five research institutes and two universities

Technology transfer, from developed to developing world

- Dutch Shell trains Omanis in petroleum extraction

- Wessex Water, U.K., brings state-of-the-art sewage treatment to Botswana

Shift of manufacturing for wage cost or logistic reasons

- Canadian textile multinational sets up in Taiwan
- Ford moves engine plant closer to Central Europe

Joint ventures and mergers for access to markets

- Finns join Japanese to sell mining equipment in Pacific zone
- Swedish Mölnlycke embarks on joint venture with Hungarian Sancella to market tampons
- Banco Bilbao-Vizcaya and French partner bank swap selected main branches

Kenichi Ohmae, head of McKinsey in Tokyo, has advocated a success strategy for international companies and has given it the label Triad. This means being a major presence in the three world centers of the United States, Europe and Japan. The only way to succeed is to establish insider status in all three, collaborating with former competitors, recruiting and promoting local national staff, and learning about working conditions and markets.

Beyond Ohmae's Triad, two other opportunities beckon: the revitalization of Central Europe and the development of the Third World. The crystal ball is hard to read, but already industries as diverse as electricity, tobacco, chemicals and insurance have recognized that, while the developed world represents today's money, the developing countries contain the seeds of growth for tomorrow.

Other observers* describe the emergence of the "transnational" company, and with it a new management approach, treating worldwide operations as an integrated and interdependent whole. The muscle of global resources must be combined with a sensitive response to local issues and opportunities. Hong Kong Bank advertises under the slo-

---

*Christopher Bartlett, Sumantra Ghoshal, *Managing Across Borders*, Harvard, 1989.

gan "Local insight. Global outlook", while Sandoz exhorts its staff: "Think Global! Act Local!" A new buzzword is gaining currency: *glocal.*

Setting up and following through these more complex arrangements involves getting together with people to thrash out unprecedented solutions to unforeseen problems. A tight grip on the deal itself, or the ability to crunch the numbers correctly, are not enough. The business stands or falls on an understanding of the other side, what motivates them, what their priorities are and how they will change as the relationship matures. In other words, what will make them want to come back for more? What happens when you get out of the bunker, back on the airplane, face-to-face on the other's territory? The faces opposite will be from other backgrounds, other cultures than your own. Technology makes it quick and easy to make some kind of contact, but the prizes will go to those who can make *good* contact.

And more than just playing Mr. Nice Guy, making good contact means being more aware.

When a company pushes through a predatorial acquisition, it can expect to lose a number of key staff in the "victim" company. That is in the nature of things. If too many depart, leaving a worthless shell, there has been a miscalculation, or a failure of planning, on the human side. That planning is even more crucial when the target company is in another country.

There are many examples of failure, but here is an all-too-rare example of success. In 1987, Ericsson won the CGCT takeover in France against competition from Siemens and AT&T, who had been seen as joint favorites. The French ministry negotiator, announcing the winner, applauded the Swedish team as the best communicators and the only ones to have taken the cultural factor into account.

The Individual

Many people, when they leave home to do a day's work, put on a mask. The thickness of the mask varies from occupation to occupation: we all know, or can easily imagine, a piano tuner or a potter who is at one with his or her craft—maskless—and we envy such fortunates from time to time. There are certain psychometric tests, usually applied to managers, which are designed to determine how thick the subject's work mask is. The results of these tests provide valuable clues to levels of stress now and in the future. For example, the manager who travels abroad a lot, for short or long periods, is subject to stresses deeper than jet lag, overcrowded itineraries and hangovers, and is likely to have a jaded view of those stay-at-homes who say they envy such an exotic lifestyle.

Airlines understand this well. "Only by flying Club Europe to over 60 European destinations can you be sure to find the same high standards of service and care throughout the Continent". A uniform homogenized service is offered to traveling managers to help them survive the difficult transitions between home (real), work (less real), work abroad (unreal) and social life abroad (frequently quite bizarre).

Managers of many nations have given the label "Hilton Culture" to the way of life offered. Its adherents have left their roots behind, replacing native values with a bland, predictable Lowest Common Denominator in entertainment, food, conversation, dress, and even ethics. They are all putting on a mask.

- **Hans Weyrich** is a sales manager, based in Hamburg. He is a happy family man, and a regular churchgoer. When his customers fly in to talk business, they expect evening entertainment too. Top of the list is Hamburg's red light district. Hans puts on the mask.

- **Abdelaziz Sabri** is also religious, and Islam prescribes fatalism. He puts on the mask when he leaves Cairo to attend production conferences within the multinational corporation that employs him: what could be less fatalistic than to talk of business targets?

- **Vera Barany,** a qualified auditor, is accustomed to the demands of central authority in a centrally planned economy. Budapest now marches to an entrepreneurial/opportunist drumbeat, and Vera is having to adjust her mask as she comes to terms with her new Western employer.

Insecurity flourishes when human understanding is at risk. And understanding is particularly at risk across a culture gap. To give an illusion of strength, we put on a protective mask that blocks us off from real contact. Meanwhile, the other side is similarly afraid.

Culture Check

Imagine you are going to meet someone from another country—preferably a country with which you have had some dealings. When that person talks to compatriots about *your* culture, what generalizations might he or she voice? "I've always said about the ...s, you know, that they are very ..." or "One thing you must remember about the ...s is that they almost always ...".

Jot down half-a-dozen impressions that you think the citizen of that country has about you and the people of your country.

1.

2.

3.

4.

5.

6.

There will probably be no absolutes on your list. The generalizations that your imaginary foreigner expresses about you and your compatriots will be relative. If your counterpart says that you are a mean or a generous people, this probably means that you are more mean or generous than his or her own compatriots.

Here are the results of running this exercise with a mixed group from the United States, Germany, Britain and Hungary. The participants were split into four mono-cultural groups to discuss the way they thought the other cultures perceived them.

Each group was asked to report back with six characteristics—adjectives or short phrases.

The American list:

- arrogant
- enterprising

The German list:

- punctual
- meticulous

- superficial
- money-oriented
- open
- uncultured.

- neat
- stubborn
- hard-working
- fond of beer and sauerkraut.

The British list:

- phlegmatic
- imperialist (they were the senior partners)
- isolationist
- principled
- tenacious
- drily humorous.

The Hungarian list:

- diligent
- proud
- gifted
- pessimistic
- undisciplined
- born victims.

With these 24 epithets pinned to the wall, the questions to be dealt with were: "Have we got each other, or ourselves, wrong in this or that respect?"; "Is this or that attitude actually an asset to the team?"; "Should we/can we modify this or that aspect of our behavior in the name of harmony?"

Then they started to build their team spirit.

"Flight" and "fight" follow the same channels in the human nervous system. Defensiveness switches over all too easily into aggression. Then communication can break down altogether.

As Others See Us

When we first went out into the world as adolescents, the burning question was "What do other people think of me?" The classic example is the 15-year-old boy or girl at a party, entirely convinced that all eyes are fixed on her outfit, or the enormous pimple on his nose.

As adults, we can be easily reduced to the same condition, if we are unsure of the ground rules operating in the alien culture in which we are trying to work.

Take a pen. Write your name five times. Now change hands and do it again. Unless you are ambidextrous, it feels rather uncomfortable. Awkward. Frustrating.

When you are on a long assignment abroad, in a culture with which you are unfamiliar, everything you do feels like that: buying a loaf of bread; catching a bus; crossing the street. All the everyday, familiar things still happen, but they are no longer familiar.

What Is "Normal?"

A friend's Scottish grandmother had returned from a holiday in Sweden, delighted with the hospitality she had enjoyed, the scenery she had absorbed and the few words of the language she had picked up, "...although it's not really a place I could ever feel at home in...I mean to say they're always dusting and cleaning....Mind you, it's more than I could say for some of the places I've been to...countries where there are cockroaches in the kitchen....But no, when you come down to it, I have to say *we're just about right.*"

One way to visualize your own standpoint on another culture is to draw a series of simple bell-curves. First, draw your own curve:

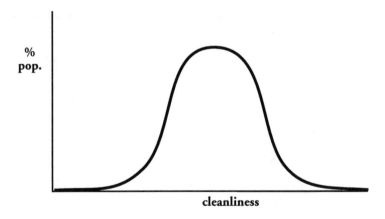

Here the middle section is normal for you in your home culture, while the areas to right and left indicate "less than you" or "more than you" of the value on the bottom axis. So the Scottish grandmother's hygiene graph would have the Swedish as abnormally to the right of the Scots.

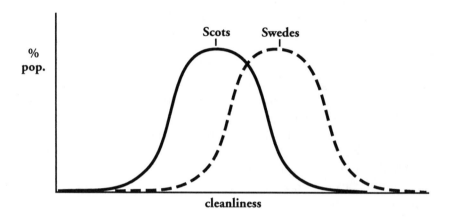

You can change the variable on the bottom axis to *punctuality*, say, or *helpfulness, loyalty* or *thoroughness*…It works best with positive attributes.

This is only a way of clarifying your own standpoint, not of learning anything new about the other culture.

Most of us are conditioned by liberal society to be ashamed of our generalized views about others. The person who trumpets views about the "differentness" of another race is considered to be an embarrassment, or dangerously ignorant, but if you are to challenge your own prejudices successfully, you must identify them as clearly as you can, and then test them against the views of others.

From Normality to Stereotype

Many, perhaps most, Britons would rather be stranded on a desert island with a German than with a Frenchman. Despite enmity in two world wars, the British and Germans believe they have certain values in common, like dependability, straightforwardness, pragmatism and a businesslike approach to life. The French and British tend to see in each other similar vices, like arrogance, selfishness and duplicity; and most Britons cannot understand the French addiction to abstract argument. All such generalizations are tendentious and gratuitous. Yet stereotypes are built on a kernel of truth...

> *The Independent*, U.K.,
> 31 March 1990

How can *The Independent* make these sweeping statements about the preferences of millions of people without including any evidence or supporting argument, and yet guess that the majority of its readers are nodding in recognition?

When it comes to a common understanding of unwritten, unspoken rules about how to get a job done or how to relax over a meal together, Germans do perhaps appear less exotic and closer to the British.

A hop across the Channel to France takes the British traveler into an atmosphere quite different from home—the fine regard for food, the sexier advertising, the nonchalant driving style. Even though this is still prime beer-drinking country, we feel we are already plugged into the Mediterranean.

Whether or not you agree about the proximity of the Germans to the British or the troubled nature of Anglo-French relations, *The Independent* is talking about something everybody knows and recognizes: our mental picture of national stereotypes.

In fact, stereotypes themselves have had a pretty bad press lately, as have their close cousins, prejudice and generalization. Anthropologists, liberal thinkers and consultants on cross-cultural affairs have been warning us: "Beware the dreaded stereotype...generalizations are vague and deceptive...prejudice condemns the foreigner without a fair hearing."

People Like to Build Barricades

On a cross-cultural awareness program run for management trainees at Shell, the participants are placed in two teams at opposite ends of an imaginary desert island. From a few scraps of information they are encouraged to build up their own "culture"—how to solve basic questions of health, wealth, power, family, etc. Then they are invited to join the other team to plan an escape from the island. This throws up a barrage of distrust, bordering on superstition, that the other team is dirty, diseased, dishonest, degenerate—and all this about the nice people they had breakfast with three hours ago!

Often, such exercises and experiments carry their own lessons for the participants—the presiding referee only has to say "Well, wasn't that interesting?" and the warning is clear: stereotypes tend to be negative stereotypes. Something in human nature prompts clannishness, and that means bad feelings towards anybody who is not "one of us".

"Good fences make good neighbors" said the poet Robert Frost. But the powerful winds of technology and economics are flattening those fences. We have to learn to work well with people who may be very different from our own tribe.

In September 1989, *Eurobusiness* magazine ran a survey of training services for managers involved in working across national frontiers. The title of the article was "Learning to Be Free of Culture". So, is the answer to jettison all stereotypes, and walk unbiased through the world, treating each person we meet as unique? Well, this might work in Utopia, but:

> The human tendency towards pattern-making is inborn and inescapable. We cannot see three dots but we make them into a triangle. Human beings have to order their experience as part of their biological adaptation to reality, and the forces which impel them to do so are just as instinctive as sex.
>
> Anthony Storr, psychiatrist

Are stereotypes more than just the result of an instinct? Are they a valid means of encapsulating experience, of joining up the dots?

The *Chambers Twentieth Century Dictionary* definition of the word stereotype is "a solid metal plate for printing cast from a mold of movable types, a fixed conventionalized representation". And the real problem with stereotypes is precisely that: they are fixed and conventionalized. They suggest a failure to learn from experience. Generalization entails leaving out the detail. And prejudice is making up your mind before you even get the experience.

A More Positive Approach

Scientists build models. Until the twentieth century, it was optimistically assumed that science progressed, step by step, nearer to the truth about nature. A scientist was supposed to collect a mass of data and then produce an eternally valid law that explained the data. The more modern view is that science sets up explanatory models which are held to be valid only until proven otherwise—until new data come along to upset the apple cart. In a universe of relativity and quantum mechanics, there is no absolute truth, only models which change or are abandoned as new information comes to light.

When you go to ask the old hand on China for advice on working there, he or she is likely to present you with just one model, the key to his or her system. As you learn to know a culture for yourself, you revise and enrich your own model of how the people in it feel, think and behave, and why they go on that way. Then you are ready to decide how best to channel your own feelings, modify your own thinking and adapt your own behavior to fit.

Goodbye Stereotypes

Stereotypes are not always based on mistakes of fact, but they do tend to mistake the part for the whole. They are often out of date, twisted by the media and popular mythology.

Above all, they make very poor small talk with the people concerned.

WE Can Say It...

In a 1979 EC Commission report on Euro-Japanese trade friction, Japanese homes were described as "what Westerners would regard as little more than rabbit hutches". This was accepted as accurate by a majority of Japanese in a survey conducted at that time by the leading newspaper *Asahi Shimbun*. The survey also showed that most disliked hearing this view expressed by foreigners. Strangely enough it was voted one of the "Ten Best Phrases of the Decade" in the same newspaper...

France: a land with a thousand sauces and only one religion. England: a land with a thousand versions of religion and only one sauce.

Italian traveler, 18th century

The British eater is generally a tolerant individual where indifferent food is concerned, yet he is unlikely to enjoy lighthearted teasing from a foreign guest about the grisly gristliness on their plates. This we might call the "mother-in-law syndrome": *I* can criticize the old lady to my heart's content, but don't *you* dare say a word against her.

Hello Models

Like a set of statistics, your model of a culture enables you to predict behavior in broad terms, but it cannot guarantee what will happen on any particular occasion. It can help you prepare for what is most likely, but may prove unreliable in any one given case. In fact, the next Texan you meet might be small, quick on his feet and modest and the next meal you eat in London might be excellent. If you roll a standard die 600 times, you'll probably score about a hundred sixes. But on the 601st throw?

Your model will give you a clear reference point, making deviations easier to understand and setting freak occurrences in context. You ad-

> ## Tell Me Another
>
> Claudia Rizzo was heading for New York to promote her bank's services. She knew her product well, and had been handpicked for her selling ability in a South Italian context. We were running her through her pitch for a particular financial service, and suggested that a certain argument could be reinforced with a concrete example of how another prestigious client had benefited from using the service (naming no names, of course). She balked. "Where I come from, if I gave a case history at a moment like that, the client would assume that I was inventing it. He wouldn't believe a word." Not in the United States, Claudia; there they expect a concrete example.

just the base model once you have accumulated enough exceptions. The model is the natural starting point. So, how do you develop and apply it?

Lessons in Model Building

Cultures are complex. Here we offer some simple approaches, to illustrate how you can use the facts you *already* know to set up a flexible model, in preparation for filtering, focusing and framing new observations.

Topography

A realtor revealed the secret of his success in a celebrated aphorism: "There are only three things that matter about a house: Location, Location and Location. Everything else can be changed." Much the same could also be said of countries.

Does the unchangeable topography of a country shape the attitudes of its people? Before you read any further, try this simple test.

Sketch a map of the United States showing state boundaries. You should have found that fairly easy. If not, you really do owe yourself a couple of hours of browsing in a school atlas!

Now do the same for Germany, showing natural and political boundaries. Mark the capital with its name. Not quite so easy, perhaps?

Even if you are German yourself, you probably hesitated for a moment at least. Recent political upheavals have greatly increased the exposure of the map of Germany in the press and on television, but the country's outline remains amorphous and unmemorable.

In fact Germany has hardly any physical boundaries. The Rhine could form one, but the actual border is further to the west. The Alps might serve, but their foothills are well inside Germany, while their heights are Swiss and Austrian. In the north, the sea coast is insignificantly short; Danish and Dutch borders lack even a molehill to distinguish them. The eastern frontier is sometimes news, sometimes history.

Lengthy articles appear in the German press there under such headings as "What does it mean to be German?" Many are intellectually unsure of the answer and that breeds emotional insecurity. There is a common saying: *"Ordnung muss sein"* ("There must be order"). That German love of order, system, structure is in part a response to the vagueness of their national borders.

A thoughtful look at the map of a country can suggest quite a lot about the attitudes of its inhabitants. Those simple outlines and contours are a good start to your model building, and give immediate coherence to the scraps of data you have in your head, or pick up

---

Don't Adjust Your Horizons Too Much

During the 70s tourist boom, Philippa was doing a summer job at the Chicago Tourist Board. She took a phone-call from London. What could she recommend for a two-day stopover in Chicago? Well, there was a lot to see...Did the caller have any personal preferences?

"Well, I figured on the first morning I might rent a car and drive to the Grand Canyon..."

Religius

during casual observation. Understanding a country for business purposes is largely a matter of unlocking and shaping the knowledge that you already have. The map itself will get you asking the right questions and equip you with a strong visual hook on which to hang the answers.

In some cases, similar landscapes yield very different results. For example, the American southwest has much in common with Mexico physically: arid, empty cactus- and petroleum-bearing land. Yet the economics, the personality and the business style of Mexico barely resemble the money, the mores or the manners of Texas and Arizona. Obviously, many other elements—religion, politics, history—go into the mix. Topography does not determine what the people are like; it is a significant contributor to their make-up, and gives you a handy tool to think with. There are other tools available.

A last word on geographical position from the Mexicans themselves, who sum up their situation thus: "Tan lejos de Dios, tan cerca de los Estados Unidos" ("So far from God, so close to the U.S.").

Religion

Another model-building instrument, a lens through which to scrutinize the attitudes of a people, is religion. The first example is that of Islam in the Arab world. What we have to say is centered on the Arabic-speaking countries—the crucible of Islam—but certain points transcend geography, and hold true for Pakistan, Indonesia, Muslim Africa and elsewhere.

We will take a couple of simple central facts, and see how they can help to build up a model of a people's standpoint and outlook.

The word Islam means submission

In other words, submission to the will of Allah. This takes us straight to a primary attitude in Islamic society. It is a deep and complex issue, and we cannot go into it here in detail. But it is an issue which can cause tension where Muslims do business with Westerners, who see business as a matter of controlling events, of applying willpower and planning to meet goals.

There is an Arabic saying: "Whoever looks into the future is either insane or irreligious". "Insha'allah" (God willing) is one of the first phrases that visitors to the Middle East pick up. It is tagged on to the end of every statement about future events, from accepting a dinner invitation to agreeing to a deadline on a construction project.

The life of the prophet Muhammad himself was full of vigorous activity, so it is clear that "submission" does not mean passivity. There is a story of a Bedouin, who listens closely as Muhammad explains that all things are in the hands of Allah, then asks: "Is there any need for me to tether my camels at night to stop them wandering?" The Prophet replies: "Tie them up firmly! Then Allah will make sure they stay put!"

A devout Muslim spoke to us about the marketing plans for which he was responsible. "Do you find any difficulty", we asked, "in gearing yourself up to push for targets in the future, when your religion dictates otherwise?" "No problem," he replied, "so long as I am working in a team with other Muslims. Together we find the right approach. The difficulty comes when I am working closely with Americans and Europeans. They see the future in such a different way."

Koran means recitation

According to some traditions, the Prophet did not write; the words of the Koran, coming direct from Allah through the Prophet's mouth, were written down by attendant scribes. One aim of traditional Islamic education has always been to learn the words of the Koran by heart. Even those who fall short of learning it in its entirety are equipped with a wealth of quotations and a highly developed oral memory.

In Middle Eastern business dealings today, there is prestige and pleasure to be gained from eloquence; good use of language (preferably Arabic, but also other tongues) is admired. Deals—and differences—are settled by talking. Written communication and contracts— "pieces of paper written all over"—come a poor second.

Ireland—"The Confessional State"

Those promoting tourism to Ireland emphasize the easygoing charm of the people you will meet there, and the general absence of pressure in the Irish way of life. There is an Irish saying: "When the good Lord created time, he created plenty of it." Irish society is fairly forgiving of lackadaisical attitudes. There is an undercurrent of belief, instilled in the country's predominantly Catholic primary schools, that a forgiving God will accept a sincere act of contrition for venial trans-gressions, and so the transgressor, once having made "a good con-fession", can start with a clean sheet.

These attitudes are not necessarily related to the devoutness or oth-erwise of the individual. Even the most down-to-earth Dublin busi-nessperson, working hard to keep an enterprise alive, is given frequent reminders of the Catholic background from which he or she sprang. Many adoptive Dubliners receive frequent letters from mother, aunt or sister in the country, liberally sprinkled with "DV" and "DG" (ab-breviations for the Latin forms of "God willing" and "thanks be to God").

Such reminders fuel the "Why worry?" attitude that foreigners often find so beguiling, and which often exasperates those Irish peo-ple who are trying to play life's game by more rigorous rules. The na-tive/Catholic Irish identify a zealous adherence to rules and timetables with those alien English who dominated Irish life for centuries.

However, Roman Catholicism among Irish (or Italian, or Polish) migrants to the United States has not engendered such carefree atti-tudes. As a formative influence, religion cannot be entirely separated from our next category, history.

History
How close to Ellis Island?

It's what America is. It's a nation of immigrants. It's the central event of American history.

Gary Roth, Manager, Ellis Island
Project

A great many Americans have an indirect memory of hunger in their family history. Their forebears survived the Atlantic and the ignominy of immigration control on New York's Ellis Island to participate in "the American way"—material self-improvement through hard work in a huge free market. There was little time for doubt or hesitation with a farm to win from the wilderness, installments to keep up on the de-livery truck, the English language to master and a growing family to provide for.

The following generation—whenever the parents arrived, and from whichever European port—was brought up with those same gritty values. Most now had shoes and full bellies; those who flourished gave priority to their own children's future well-being—through education and through access to the good things in life. (A running theme in American family humor has been the exasperation of the first- or second-generation father at the financial demands of his children.) By the third or fourth generation, a visceral need to succeed in the New World gives way to nostalgia for family roots in the Old.

When dealing with a white American, it is useful to determine what generation he or she represents. Is Europe the malevolent, prejudiced, no-opportunity hell from which their parents escaped, or the quaint, culturally rich home where their great-great grandparents grew up?

For Europeans, the "American" businessperson usually means the New York businessperson, scion of a family that did not join the westward trail, a member of an ethnic group within that cosmopolitan city. The closer that businessperson feels to Ellis Island, the more likely he or she is to be a tough, win-lose negotiator, shamelessly in pursuit of the Almighty Dollar.

Two layers of Bulgarian history

There are two layers of history to consider when visiting Bulgaria: Turkish domination, which ended 120 years ago, and Soviet Communist influences on the last three generations.

When building your model of a post-Stalinist society, it is important to ask: "Is this happening because of something ancient in this culture, or because of the habits of the Centrally-Planned Economy?"

Topography, Religion and History

We will now briefly consider the cultural make-up of the "typical" Japanese businessperson, Toshi Suzuki by name, to determine how topographical, demographic, religious and historical threads are woven together in Toshi's attitudes.

Most people know that Japan is overcrowded (only 30 per cent of the landmass being habitable). Few westerners recognize the historical aspect of this topographical truth: the fertile coastal strip of Japan has been packed solidly with humanity for many hundreds of years. There is no Japanese word for "privacy", unless we admit the imported *"puraibashi"*. Like his ancestors, Toshi must find ways of getting some privacy without the benefit of a solid bedroom door to close behind him.

Those ancestors despised and feared foreigners. For over 250 years (the Tokugawa era), while Western European cultures were evolving liberal democracies, Japan remained cut off in its feudalism—until 1868.* The echoes of xenophobia and a need for clear hierarchy are still strong in Toshi's life.

The third thread is religion—or rather the lack of it. At the beginning of the Tokugawa period, all religious and philosophical works were banned—except the Analects of Confucius. The permitted code was a mercilessly rigid pecking order, a system of conduct based on duty (*giri*) as opposed to individual human rights, and a relativist ethical outlook—no Ten Commandments recited from the pulpit in nineteenth-century Japan. Behavior was, and still is for Toshi, largely determined by the company being kept.

Toshi learned at his mother's knee to modify his language according to the status of those present; he is under constant social pressure to keep his emotions to himself; his employers encourage ever more dedication to the harmony of the group.

✝ Making Connections

Each of these cultural sketches outlined above contains a few basic facts. More important are the connections drawn within each piece between those background facts and the attitudes typical of the culture in question. As this book progresses, we shall consider how such attitudes affect behavior, particularly in business, and suggest how you

---

*In 1853, the U.S. Navy forced Japan to open its gates to international trade. This led directly to the collapse of the Tokugawa order.

Culture Check

1. Try to extrapolate from the following background facts a pattern of attitudes in the people who come from the countries listed:

> Finland—lakes and forests;
> Hungary—landlocked;
> Belgium—two languages;
> England—Industrial Revolution
> India—the caste system;
> Peru—land of the Incas;
> Canada—the northern neighbor of the United States.

2. Experiment with another analytical instrument. Take a culture you know quite well, and see what patterns emerge when you look at it through a pair of spectacles borrowed from a meteorologist.

For example, does Swedish introspection have anything to do with long, dark winters? When a North Italian calls southerners unreliable, is it connected with the sunshine?

3. Let your curiosity take new paths.

- A colleague of ours, unversed in the ways of Islam, read in draft the paragraphs about the Koran and the oral tradition. She immediately asked: "Do the women in Islamic cultures share in this passion for eloquence, or is it a male preserve?"

- Our "Ellis Island" model was challenged by a Puerto Rican, who quite reasonably accused us of oversimplification. A fuller essay on the United States would need research on the ethnic groups which did not travel from Europe. How does the *facts/attitudes/behavior* sequence apply to them?

- Once you have started to build your model of a culture, you can augment and enrich it by asking questions of it, challenging it, thinking laterally. And by having fun with it!

might modify your own behavior accordingly—improving your chances of reaching your business goals.

Building flexible models upward from *facts*, through *attitudes*, to *behavior* is more useful than accumulating random "handy hints" regarding business cultures. It helps to know that a Japanese business card should be received in both hands and venerated, or that your Arab business partner might be offended if you pass something with your left hand. But such snippets of good manners mean a lot more if they can be set in a context.

The Story of Lucy

There is a river. Beside the river, in a little house, lives Lucy. Lucy is in love with Peter (who lives on the other side of the river), and she doesn't know what to do. So she goes to her friend William and asks him.

"Perfectly simple," says William. "If you love him, go and tell him." "OK", says Lucy, and she goes to the river, where she meets David, the boatman. "Please will you take me across the river, David?"

"Of course. But what time do you want to come back again?"

"I don't really know", Lucy confesses. "Why do you ask?" David explains that he has a contract downriver at six o'clock, and that if Lucy wants a ferry home, she must be at the landing stage before that time.

They cross the river. Lucy goes to Peter's house and knocks on the door. Peter opens the door. Lucy says, "Peter, I love you." Peter cannot resist the temptation. He makes love to Lucy.

When she recovers from her delirium, Lucy becomes upset at the thought that Peter has taken advantage of her. She runs out of the door, along beside the river, and to the house where Michael lives.

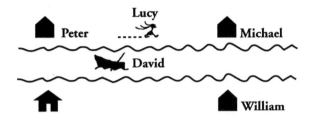

Now, Michael is in love with Lucy, so when he opens the door and sees her there so clearly troubled, he says, "Come in, you poor girl, and tell me all about it." Lucy goes in and tells him all about it. Michael becomes upset in his turn, and asks Lucy to leave.

She arrives at the landing stage at one minute past six. David has cast off, and is rowing away from the jetty. Lucy calls to him, "David, please will you take me home?" David points to his watch. "I'm sorry, Lucy. I warned you." And he rows away downstream.

Lucy decides to swim home. In midstream, she drowns.

There are five characters in this story. Your job now is to rank them, one to five, in descending order of responsibility for the death of Lucy. In other words, if you think Michael is the most responsible, enter him in slot 1, and work your way down.

1   _____

2   _____

3   _____

4   _____

5   _____

Commentary

This is an old Victorian smoking-room exercise—the sort of thing gentlemen diverted themselves with over brandy and cigars when the ladies had withdrawn after dinner.

The key to the game is primitive, and bears little relation to any modern psychological theory. Thus warned, read on.

Each of the five characters in the story represents a human quality. The order in which you rank them reflects the importance that you attach to each of those qualities. The lower on the scale of responsibility, the more important that characteristic is to you. If you blame character X for Lucy's death, you are saying that you despise or reject his motives.

Cast in order of appearance:

Lucy	represents	*Love;*
William	represents	*Wisdom;*
David	represents	*Duty;*
Peter	represents	*Passion;*
Michael	represents	*Morality* (or so the Victorians felt. Why do you think he kicked Lucy out? Your interpretation reflects your culture.)

So, according to the rules of the game, if you decided on the ranking:

William
Peter
Lucy
Michael
David

you attach little importance to wisdom and a great deal to duty.

Of course, you project a lot into the story as you read it: How old was Lucy in your mind's eye? Was the river a stream with ducks on it, or an icy torrent? When she called out to David, was she pleading with tears in her eyes?—We never said so.

Cross-Cultural Interpretation

Ponder for a moment how cultural background might affect a person's responses to the sad tale of Lucy.

We have run this exercise many times on training courses, with groups of mixed nationality. On one notable occasion, the participants in the test were nine Swedes and three Venezuelans, all working for the same company, whose headquarters is in Stockholm. The Scandinavians (men and women) unanimously placed Lucy at the head of the list, while the South Americans all had her at the foot ("But poor little Lucy!").

And the same spread was true in Italy, where none of the Neapolitans in the group could see Loving Lucy as anything more than a helpless victim, to the bemusement of their Milanese colleagues—who agreed with each other that she should have shown more sense, and deserved her fate.

Similarly, David (Duty) is usually placed high on the list by Latins ("For a lousy contract he condemns a beautiful girl to death!"). The classic German response is that he had a job to do, that he gave Lucy fair warning, and that he made the right decision in the circumstances. (*"Ordnung muss sein"*). Yet within Germany, there is likely to be disagreement between, say, a young Bavarian and an older Prussian.

Some say, when asked to allocate responsibility for Lucy's death, that there is simply not enough evidence to go on. (Perhaps you reacted that way yourself.) This shortage of data often leads to what we call "The Lawyer's Answer", placing Lucy herself first (she was alone when she died), followed by David (the last to see her before the drowning), and then Michael, Peter, and William (in reverse order of appearance in the story as told). In our experience, the Cartesian-minded French person is likely to choose this option.

William rarely gets the blame: few people say "It was his fault—he started it all." There was a Swiss-German once who guessed that the rest of the group would place Lucy first for what he considered to be liberal/feminist reasons. He succeeded in provoking them by blaming William above all, on the grounds that "he missed his opportunity".

And of course, culture changes over time. Western women now not only hear the story of Lucy without blushing, but place her top of the list as responsible for her own actions.

Value Grid

Now here is a simple way of crystallizing a model of another culture and comparing it to your own.

In the following table Column 1 is for your own culture, Column 2 is for a culture you know fairly well, and Column 3 is for a culture you know only a little.

Put the names of those cultures at the top of the columns.

Next, picture in your mind ten people from your home culture who are more or less your social equivalents—similar age, similar education, similar occupation. Now look at Question 1, Column 1. If you think four of the compatriots you have chosen go regularly to church (or mosque, or temple, or shrine), enter "40%" in the box.

Now picture a group of "similar" people from your chosen culture in Column 2, and enter a percentage. And so on. Sometimes you will have knowledge to support your scoring, sometimes you will be relying on intuition or guesswork.

Commentary

As you filled in the form, you were making certain assumptions about what the questions meant regarding your "home culture". You probably transferred something of those assumptions to the "foreign" cultures.

If you are from Caracas, travel often in the United States, and have never met a Greek, you know with some precision how Venezuelan middle managers view their companies. You have made a reasoned estimate of the same value among your North American partners, and pondered your ignorance about the Greek attitude.

This exercise is useful as a framework for identifying such areas of ignorance. You are reasonably equipped to do business in a foreign culture when you have a clear view on at least half the questions.

	Home culture	Known culture	Little-known culture
1. Active in religious observance	%	%	%
2. Materially ambitious	%	%	%
3. Family-minded as priority	%	%	%
4. Fond of alcohol as social lubricant	%	%	%
5. Earnest about the company	%	%	%
6. Mobile from job to job	%	%	%
7. International in outlook	%	%	%
8. In awe of authority	%	%	%
9. Respectful of qualifications	%	%	%
10. Egalitarian/ feminist	%	%	%

CHAPTER TWO

Company

During your dealings with them, your business partners will be the embodiment of their company, division or department. Consider how their "company culture" is different from yours, and what you might do to bridge that gap.

Make all your decisions as if you owned the company.

> Robert Townsend, former president
> of Avis

Company Culture

Many executives are involved in international business without much understanding of market forces. We cannot step up to the second level of our pyramid without finding out about the markets in which we are operating. Markets operate in the context of "Culture", and set the context for "Company".

The entrepreneur, managing his or her own affairs from top to bottom, cannot afford to ignore such factors. If you are a cog in a bigger machine, you can only gain if you emulate the successful entrepreneur.

Questionnaire

The following questionnaire is a simple microscope to help you look at your company (or your supplier's, or your customer's, or your competitor's, or your banker's...), and perhaps find some pattern in the movements of the bacilli on the slide. What factors underlie the behavior of employees?

In completing the questionnaire, bear Townsend's advice in mind: place yourself in the position of the CEO, or guiding spirit of the corporation, and answer the questions as he or she would.

After the quiz, we will report on how executives from various companies have responded to it.

For each section you have a total of ten points to distribute among the statements (a), (b) and (c). The points can be spread over two or three statements, or you can concentrate on a single one.

The questionnaire is written in the first person ("my company...", "we have subsidiaries..."), but remember it can be applied to another company—perhaps the one you are about to have dealings with.

In Column 1, enter "the way my company really is"; Column 2 is for "the way my company should be", or "the way my company seems to be going"; in Column 3 you can put in scores for "the other company".

1. My company is efficient because: 1 | 2 | 3
   (a) we set up the right systems
   (b) we trust our people
   (c) we are flexible and responsive to client needs

2. We hire the right people because: 1 | 2 | 3
   (a) managers involved in recruitment have good
       judgment
   (b) we define precisely the type of person we want
   (c) candidates are helped to understand the val-
       ues of the people they would be working with
       before they decide to join

3. We handle public relations successfully because: 1 | 2 | 3
   (a) we have a clear sense of our identity
   (b) we have an open door to clients and press
   (c) we make efforts to get a message across to the
       community and the market

4. We solve problems and make decisions: 1 | 2 | 3
   (a) by thinking things over in isolation
   (b) by going to the right specialist
   (c) by pooling ideas from many sources

5. Innovation in products and organization: 1 | 2 | 3
   (a) is not a primary concern; we are already lead-
       ers in our field
   (b) is a challenge; our past and present success
       can make change more difficult
   (c) is a natural process; our current success stim-
       ulates new approaches

6. Top management get results because: 1 | 2 | 3
   (a) there is one strong person who makes all the
       crucial decisions
   (b) there is a group of experienced people at the
       top who know where the firm is heading
   (c) it is receptive to signals from outside and from
       below

7. Leadership throughout our organization is effective because: 1 | 2 | 3
   - (a) managers give clear, detailed instructions and monitor progress closely
   - (b) managers work closely with their teams and set the right example
   - (c) managers set clear goals but let subordinates decide how to reach them
8. Human relations are good because: 1 | 2 | 3
   - (a) we do not mix business with pleasure
   - (b) we socialize mainly with our peers
   - (c) senior and junior people feel free to relax together
9. Our activities are international in that: 1 | 2 | 3
   - (a) we export a lot
   - (b) we have marketing outlets in other countries
   - (c) we have subsidiaries with full functions in other countries
10. We are an international team in that: 1 | 2 | 3
    - (a) we employ local staff abroad for some functions
    - (b) operations abroad are led and managed by local nationals
    - (c) the corporate board includes members from many countries

Commentary and Findings

The questionnaire above draws heavily on *Beyond Negotiation* by Carlisle and Parker. We used it as a basis for interviews with about a hundred managers from various industries and countries.

We set out with the following thesis, derived in part from Carlisle and Parker: a company with the right culture will have an advantage in international competition; the right culture is one that favors creativity, fairness and open communication.

We half expected the underlying theme to be obvious to the respondents: surely most of them would point to option (c) in every case and say "that is where my company would like to be". In fact, the results were far more complex, giving some indication of the diversity that people bring to the business of running a business.

The results, from which we present a selection below, also support the theme of this book: *business cultures are deeply embedded in country cultures.*

(*Note:* The companies and our respondents preferred to remain anonymous.)

Respondent A: Frenchwoman providing support to front-line bankers in international work at the Paris branch of a U.S. bank.

1. Corporate culture plays a big part in our bank. On joining, at any level, everybody goes through a one-week seminar about the aims, the driving force, the history of the bank. And there's a motto about quality which is pushed quite hard. We operate in a specific niche with top-rank clients only. We have to fit our service precisely to what the client wants—tailored solutions. So even junior people, who may never see the client, have to understand this special approach.

2. We do a lot to get this approach across to people before they join. Satisfying the client is very hard work, which not everybody wants. There are plenty of easier jobs. But here you get the chance to follow your own initiative and to work with highly motivated colleagues. Definition plays a part, too: we need people with good contacts in the market, which includes, for example, graduates of the top business schools.

3. Within the bank there's a strong sense of belonging, in both a local and a global sense. People like to talk about how old-established we are, what we did in the crash of 1929. It's rather surprising for the French, who tend to have a more individualist attitude to work. The French style is to be dedicated to the profession and the career, rather than the corporation. The bank does no cold selling and only advertises selectively; we work through contacts and connections and build up long-term relations.

4. Networking and pooling of experience flow freely, even from one country to another. The overall structure for decisions is that each subsidiary has a wide measure of freedom, but must

report upwards in great detail. The same goes for each department or team within the subsidiary.

5. Adapting to the client means constant innovation. That's the heart of the business. Our services are expensive—if we don't come up with new ideas, our clients will go elsewhere.

6. Top management at the U.S. end are quite visible. We know their names and most of the faces. When someone new joins the board, we get a big memo, describing his or her career and aims. Until recently, there was a single strong man at the top. He was particularly good at representing the bank, almost a symbolic leader, though also very receptive. What we see currently is a strong group in control.

7. At my level, I can solve some problems myself, but I can also go up for advice without any loss of face. I can call a senior person in the United States, once, but not too often. If need be, I can ask my superior in Paris to use his authority to help me.

8. In spite of the sense of belonging, human relations are not always that smooth. The atmosphere is highly competitive. A lot of young people have been brought in recently and there's rivalry among them. On top of that is a generation gap with the 40- and 50-year-olds who joined in easier times. They're still needed for cultural continuity. But there are tensions which you must expect in a fast-moving climate.

9. Our market positioning means we are fully present in the world's financial capitals, but not at all outside them. We have no presence in the Third World. And our experiments with offices in the French provinces didn't lead anywhere. Our customers are either in the big city, or they like to come there.

10. The subsidiaries are led by locals, but with very close reporting to the United States. The board was 100 percent American until very recently when an Englishman made it. That was quite a breakthrough.

Respondent B: British manager in the central office of a petroleum multinational.

1. We've been fortunate—it's a good business to be in, and many of our high-risk opportunities have paid off. Demand may fluctuate, but it's always there, and on a far greater scale than could have been dreamed of when the company first began. We have a long history and we take a long-term view. With a 5-year rolling plan and a scenario that extends 20 years ahead, we really do have a strong vision of the future. Systems, yes, but that suggests something too rigid. There's a set of business principles, a way of projecting a vision from the center, giving people confidence to make the right decision.

2. It takes a long time to build a chief executive. Potential executives have to pick up an awful lot in a short time, if they're going to be effective as top managers by their late 40s. Say a candidate has had 25 years in the company—that's very little indeed in a long-term business like ours. It's unlikely that you'll reach the very top unless you start early. So we have to pick the very best and we pick them young. Recruitment tends to look for "people like us", though some mavericks do slip through and serve an important leavening function.

3. It's a commodity business, but a highly competitive one. That means image really counts. The way we handle PR affects our business performance very directly: for example, in getting government support at the exploration stage; raising capital in financial markets; even cash sales at the petrol pump. The wrong move or the wrong message on sensitive issues like the environment could make mincemeat of a lot of carefully-made plans.

    I would say we're good with the institutions, with professionals and probably with schools too. We're less consistent with the public at large—which is the most complicated. But we maintain a healthy market share, and that suggests we're reasonably well regarded.

4. There's a kind of looseness in the way we go about making decisions—it can seem tedious at times, but it can also work miracles. On a major issue, the end of the process will be unanimous acceptance. Underlying the consensus is that central vision of where the company is going. For most matters

there are specialists within the company, but we have called in outside consultants, for example, on the issue of organizational change.

5. Innovation on the product side is evolutionary, and we spend heavily on research. But the business environment has changed dramatically and we've had to change the organization to meet it. The "Seven Sisters"* no longer have predominance in the industry. We're now in competition with the producer nations themselves. The era of country club culture and straight-line economic projections is over. We have to be more flexible, more open.

6. We have good antennae: lots of people constantly listening for signals all around the world. Authority is delegated to the operating countries. It's non-autocratic.

7. Signals get passed, often through informal networks. I'll pass a message to someone overseas to think, to follow a lead from that central vision. It might be just a question "What have you done about that?" or advice like "This is unlikely to gain support". Because managers move around a lot, a powerful network builds up. People get to know each other and that aids communication.

8. There's a loyalty common to all and a fair deal for everyone. The wife of one of our senior managers in China, who disappeared during the Cultural Revolution and spent many years in jail, recently turned up in our Hong Kong office. Everything was laid on for her, pension on tap, she was "one of us". In Eastern Europe, there are people drawing pensions from us who were on the payroll before the Second World War. It's all part of the long-term view.

9. It was an international company from the very start. Today, we have more interests in more countries than any of our competitors. Shareholders are also very widely spread around the world.

---

*BP, Chevron, Esso, Gulf, Mobil, Shell, Texaco.

10. Posting managers to different countries is part of their training and a way of consolidating the communication network. There are many nationalities working at central office, as well. In my case, I'm British, with other nationalities directly senior and junior to me. All this leads to speedier decisions and, I believe, better decisions. Movement may mean losing some depth and client contact, but it means we can call on a very rich pool of talent. For a decisive post, we can match not only qualifications and experience, but temperament—we can bring in a market-builder, a consolidator, a soft-spoken diplomat, or whatever, from anywhere in the world. The original nationality of the company has been almost lost in this international melting pot.

Respondent C: A fast-track 25-year-old with four years in a Swiss financial services company, just getting his first taste of responsibility.

1. Setting up systems seems less important in a mature company like ours. We have to trust people; the way we're organized means a lot of travel. So the person on the spot *is* the company.

2. The company's prestige used to be a big factor in the recruitment game, but that's less important now that other companies are boosting their images and their training programs. A "good nose" is not a very Swiss quality, but that is essential in fast-moving times. The company is recruiting younger people than before—they learn faster and cost less. These days, learning speed is more valuable than experience.

3. We do have an open door on general matters, making results of our research available, but without a heavy promotion angle. On internal matters, we are not open at all. There were some hiccups recently among top management. Of course I can't tell you what. That's very Swiss.

4. Team decisions are the norm. We have lots of specialists (inside the company) and go to them with problems, but not for decisions. Decisions are to do with finding consensus. Everyone must feel comfortable with the decision.

5. There is a bit of a generation war on "innovation". Swiss people of a certain age tend to get complacent. They've estab-

lished their way of doing things, their circle of friends in the company, jokes in common. Naturally they don't embrace big changes readily. For younger management, it's a challenge.

6. There are no high-profile leaders. Look at Swiss politics; we haven't had a charismatic leader since Wilhelm Tell. The flow of information to the top is good.

7. When you start, it's detailed monitoring for a year or so, then lots of advice for the next two or three. After that, you're on your own. For the boss, it's obvious from the year-end results whether you're on the right track.

8. Traditionally, business and pleasure have been quite separate, but among the under 30s there's quite a lot of friendship which spills over outside the office. There is very little social contact up the hierarchy. I've socialized four times in four years with my boss.

9. Basically we are exporters, though in the special sense of financial services. Outside the major financial capitals, we are light on the ground and do a lot of traveling.

10. In the few foreign establishments we do have, day-to-day management is in local hands. It would be hard to imagine a foreigner anywhere near the top of the company.

Respondent D: Board member, Spanish manufacturing company.

1. We are something like an industrial boutique, specialists in high quality product, limited volumes, near the top of the price range. But we set out 20 years ago with a very different aim: to build the world's largest factory in our sector. The crisis years of the 1970s put a stop to that, and subsequent deregulation kept up the pressure. Massive staff cuts had to be put through in a climate of fear. Just as a serious illness can make you give up your bad old habits, a few of us clearly saw the need for a new way of thinking. What came in was quality, open communications, commitment to training.

2. For the last 15 years, it's been mainly reverse recruitment, laying people off. All done on a straight seniority formula

agreed upon with the unions. The average age of the work-force is now around 45. Currently, we hardly recruit at all. If we do, we're more interested to know *their* values than to explain ours.

3. As we're a subsidiary, our parent has the main PR responsibility. It's out of our hands and we're not always happy with the way they handle it. But the market is aware of our quality.

   Within the company, the quality programs have built a strong sense of identity. There are 56 quality circles in a work-force of 1500. An effective detail is the suggestion box for slogans, which are then used around the plant, in the local press or even on the product. But an open door policy is something I don't believe in.

4. In a crisis, thinking matters more than acting. We found our own way through the crisis of the 1970s. Consultants are there to get your own ideas well presented or to do dirty work in a clean and polished style. We bring in technical advice from outside, and, like the Japanese, we go and look round our competitors. The Japanese imitate with ease themselves, but they are not easy to imitate.

5. Ideally, innovation flows like a stream. In reality, it's a tough job. In our business, investment decisions are politically sensitive, often linked to regional policies. Our organization is changing continuously, and with the minimum of formalities. The true organigram is best kept in a locked drawer or, better still, in the managers' minds.

6. In stormy weather, we've learned that a powerful captain is essential. A committee can lose the ship. But the captain must be sensitive to signals; otherwise, you end up going full speed in the wrong direction.

7. Spaniards hate being told what to do. As a people, we're the opposite of the Japanese—each person thinks he or she is a leader. The only way to get acceptance is to explain the reasons why you want something done.

   Different leadership styles fit different levels in the company. Near the top, the rule is (c)—set the goals and let people reach them in their own way. In the middle, leadership is closely linked to training and coaching, so it's (a). On or near the factory floor, it's (b): the leader has to be physically close to the team and involved with them in detail. To summarize: at the top, the question is where to go; in the middle, it's where to go and how to get there; at the bottom it's how to get there.

8. Human relations are good because we tell the truth. And the truth has to be clear and understandable. For example, the rule-book requires us to distribute our balance sheet. But I know there's little point. I'm happy to hand it to an economist, because that's someone who'll understand it. If I give it to everyone, they'll just think I'm trying to confuse them.

    We used to play soccer with the workers, but I nearly got my leg broken, so I said "Forget it. If you've got a grievance, bring it to me in my office. Don't kick my shins."

    One thing which I'm especially proud of—well, I thank God who made me excellent!—is our special open day. Heavy industry in Spain is very divided on sex lines: work is for the man, home is for the woman. We open up one day per year to the wives and children, so they can see what their husbands and fathers are doing, how the factory works, what the end product is. That makes them proud—and the fathers, too. Spanish pride may be a fault or a virtue, but management has to address it.

9. Most of our output goes to Spanish industry, but our customers may well ship our stuff to their other factories in Germany or France. We also supply direct to other countries in the EC. Do we still call that export? I'm not so sure.

10. Everyone on the payroll is Spanish.

Respondent E: Scientist reporting to top management in a German pharmaceutical firm.

1. New conditions call for a new kind of manager. Change is now so rapid and unpredictable, both in our markets and in the political scene which shapes them. Look what's happened to Germany in the last 12 months. Traditionally, German managers, especially in scientific fields, have been planners;

they work in a regulatory environment which encourages them to play safe. But the new manager must be able to cope with the unpredictable, with "chaos", with creativity. We've been putting a lot of thought into this just recently: systems have to be there, but the client is the motor.

2. Personnel work is very decentralized. Each manager is largely responsible for his or her own team, for recruiting and developing the right people.

3. PR is an emotional area. We've gone in for a new corporate identity package—logo and so on—but we find we have to do more these days. Social pressures, especially the environment issue, mean that quality and know-how no longer speak for themselves.

4. We don't have the pyramid organization you'll find in larger German companies. Teamwork is the way. But who can you hang if things go wrong? We're always balancing between accountability on the one hand and freedom to take risks on the other.

5. Innovation is our lifeblood. Twenty-five percent of turnover goes into R&D. It's a challenge, but not because of complacency. It takes eight years or more to develop a new drug; then we have a ten-year payback period in the market before the patent runs out. So we're under constant pressure, not only to find the new products, but to work more swiftly and to anticipate the market of the future.

6. The team approach includes the top management. Bottom-up communication is easy and most new proposals start from below. But it could change: in times of crisis, you need a strong leader—just as the Romans used to appoint a dictator for war.

7. Expertise is respected, because of the business we're in, and the right knowledge can outweigh rank. For example, I have to make an evaluation: should the company enter a certain new field? While it's going on, it's completely confidential to me and my team. No big boss can come and ask for details (once something escaped, you'd never get the genie back in

the bottle). When I present my conclusions, the boss might have been thinking "Yes", but I'm saying "No". There'd be some discussion, a postponement to save the boss's face, but the final decision would be "No".

8. During working hours, social contact is pretty relaxed. We all eat in the same canteen. Outside work, just where friendships happen to spring up—not a great deal between different levels.

9/10. It's a private company with worldwide sales. Marketing offices are in perhaps a hundred countries, but full-blown subsidiaries are only in a few key markets. Those are managed by locals. At heart it's a German company. You won't see many foreign faces at HQ canteen.

Respondent F: Personnel manager in a major Japanese utility company.

1. We're very people-oriented. Subordinates do feel that their bosses trust them, that good performance will be seen and lead to promotion. The seniority system in Japanese companies means everyone can expect promotion, even automatic promotion, up to a certain level. But the road to the very top is only for the very few. Only the real profit producers will get there. Everyone has the dream that it could be them. The automatic promotion system encourages that dream, makes us all work harder, even in unsatisfactory working conditions. This is true of almost all big Japanese companies.

2. Job definitions are very loose. The Japanese way is to hire the person, then train them as needed for the jobs that arise. The Western way is rather to define the job and then hire a person to fit it. In Japan we look for general talent with plenty of job rotation and training to prepare people for more senior posts.

3. We've invested heavily in making our name known. We can say that it's been successful, but there is still some question as to whether the expenditure was really worthwhile.

4. Consultation is very important to our decision making, with

plenty of face-to-face, one-to-one contact. During this stage decisions can be quite tough. Once consensus is reached, there is a meeting to announce it, which is just a formality.

5. Innovation is natural. Shareholder pressure forces us to keep our customers happy and that means constantly bringing in new ideas.

6. It's a group approach at the top and, as in all big companies, there's a risk of bureaucracy. In fact they're becoming more open to signals.

7. Teamwork is the rule. Contact with my immediate superior is frequent, though never familiar. The one above him I hardly contact at all.

8. We go drinking together in the evening and when we run out of business topics we'll chat about sports, hobbies, family—but wives never appear. Home entertaining is difficult: Japanese homes are far from work and rather small. I might get invited to my boss's home once a year at most.

9/10. As we are a utility, international steps are limited—by the nature of the business and by law. Even so, we send a dozen or so people each year to the United States and Europe for education and training.

In conclusion

Corporate culture, and the analysis of it, has been much in fashion in recent years. Currently on the market are a range of detailed diagnostics, enabling you to map every twist in your corporate nature. Our aim is simpler. The ten points in the questionnaire should start to clarify your thoughts about your own company. More important is to start thinking about your partner's company: how do *they* make decisions? What kind of deals and relationships will attract *them*? What style of communication will they best understand?

Culture Check

A Little Light Reading

Your company has a subsidiary in the imaginary land of Garundia, and you have been asked to go there for a two-week visit—"Have a look around, get to know the people, come back and make proposals for improved communication."

You know nothing about the place ("very valuable—look at the set-up through fresh eyes"), so you book a briefing session with George, an old Garundia hand, for the day before your departure. In preparation for that, you study last year's Annual Report from the Garundian subsidiary.

George gets sick. He telephones you:"Don't worry about a thing. Lovely people, the Garundians. If you like, you can have a look around my office—pick up a little light reading for the flight…". (In case you didn't know, the flight to Garundia takes two-and-a-half hours, wherever in the world you start from.)

Below is a list of the items you find in George's rather chaotic office. Which would you put in your briefcase, and why?

1. The "Kings and Queens" volume from the 12-volume *Children's Encyclopedia Garundica;*

2. Your subsidiary's annual report from five years ago;

3. A copy of George's entertainment expenses claim for his last visit to Garundia;

4. Last year's Annual Report from one of your local competitors in Garundia;

5. *Explain me, Please!*—a Garundian phrase book;

6. A Garundian cookbook, entitled *The Cuisine of a Cultural Crossroads;*

7. An organization chart of your Garundian subsidiary, modified in pencil by George under the heading "Who *really* does what";

8. A road map of Garundia, incorporating a street map and public transport guide for the Garundian capital;

9. A two-year-old *Wall Street Journal* supplement on Garundia;

10. *The Lightning in Summer,* by Janko Torquinel—"an action-packed historical romance set in the period of our country's birth";

11. A recent issue of *Deadline Garundia,* a glossy business monthly "showcasing all that is best in Garundian commerce and industry";

12. A catalog, in Garundian, of your company's current products.

Try this exercise with a friend. If he or she has chosen the cookbook where you have chosen the *Wall Street Journal,* you have learned something about each other's priorities.

There is no correct answer; below you will find a few of our thoughts on each of the 12 items.

1. *Children's Encyclopedia Garundica*—"Kings and Queens" volume

   This might be a bit heavy—in both senses. That said, it is probably a better bet than the adult version. Serious reference books are full of detail that is difficult to absorb, while "Did You Know?" books can be quite accurate yet digestible.

   The information itself will probably have little bearing on your business in Garundia, but it can score big points if you are able to point at the statue in the marketplace and say: "Ah, yes, that's Stig the Liberator, isn't it?"

2. Annual Report from five years ago

   You have already studied last year's, we said. By comparing the two, you might detect some rough financial trends, and determine how many promises the CEO has been keeping.

3. George's expenses claim

    Might give you some insight into levels and costs of entertaining in Garundia. It depends on how scrupulously George plays the game.

4. Competitor's annual reports

    Could be useful if you know how Garundians lay out their accounts. Or if you want to learn.

5. Phrase book

    Definitely a good idea to learn a few words of greeting on the plane.

6. Cookbook

    Some material for small talk, perhaps, but the contents may bear little resemblance to what is served in the average restaurant or canteen.

7. Annotated organization chart

    Potentially useful item. George's notes might not be totally objective, of course, but properly handled they will give you a flying start. People and their real concerns are the reason you are getting on the plane.

8. Map

    Any map can tell you a great deal about a place (*see* Chapter 1), besides helping you find your way around.

9. Old *Wall Street Journal* supplement

    Very useful, though going out of date. At that age, *Barrons* equivalent would be more valuable, giving a longer-term view.

10. *Historical romance*

    Read a few paragraphs: a pleasant way to take in a lot of cultural background, or a monumental bore? Make a note of author and title—Torquinel might be a national hero, and you might find yourself addressing

> a chamber of commerce conference in the Torquinel suite of the local Hilton.
>
> 11. Business glossy
>   Probably dull, possibly distorted, but another source of useful names.
>
> 12. Product catalog
>   Useful for picking up some vocabulary related to your field—which won't be in the phrasebook.

Hub, Spoke and Rim

...we can have sympathy for the managing director of a newly acquired subsidiary.... What is desperately needed is an account of how, whether and when the subsidiary *is* better off as part of a larger company than as an independent entity.

Michael Goold and Andrew Campbell, *Strategies and Styles*

Different international and multinational companies distribute their internal power in different ways. Yet most executives working in most companies recognize the importance and difficulty of good communications between headquarters (the hub) and far-flung subsidiaries (along the spokes of the wheel). Even more problematic is an efficient system of communications from subsidiary to subsidiary (around the rim).

The HQ-based executive, with staff in a distant subsidiary, cannot expect a creative attitude to communications around the rim unless he or she sets a good example.

There is a joke about the "corporate seagull." He flies down from his elevated perch, deposits his message on those below, and flies away again. This section is addressed to the corporate seagull who would like to be more welcome on his or her next visit.

A Cozy Picture

Imagine yourself working on a fascinating project with a colleague of similar disposition, sharing the same office.

Now build in a little *motivation* problem: your colleague ceases to pull his or her weight. That will change your relationship at least temporarily, but you have ample opportunity to talk it through and sort the problem out.

Next, promote one of you over the other, giving your colleague the opportunity to pull rank at times of disagreement. Again, the relationship will be affected, causing as many ulcers in the new "boss" as in the new "subordinate". Here you have problems of *hierarchy*.

So it might be time to move to separate offices. If you also regularly have lunch in the restaurant on the corner while your colleague uses the company cafeteria, you will be limiting *contact* to times when you have formal appointments. What are the effects on the working relationship?

Things are even more complicated if you vary the mix of *culture:* say you are a fourth generation Norwegian from the Bible Belt of the United States, while she is a New Yorker from the Lower East Side.

These differences in background and outlook can be fruitful...with luck...always supposing you have a common *language* in which to discuss them. But what if your colleague's first language is French, while you failed first grade Spanish and gave up everything but English at that point?

Such are the overlapping issues in any act of communication between the head office controller and the local manager: motivation, hierarchy, contact, culture and language.

The degree to which a company has a genuinely international style often relates directly to how much the company sells outside the home market. The South American sales director of a Swiss pharmaceuticals company had previously worked for an American competitor.

> Of course my new company is more truly international. My former employers sold 80 percent of their output within the United States: American research, American production and distribution, American consumers. So they naturally exported their American management style to deal with the other 20 percent, and expected foreign employees to conform to their ethics and practices. With the Swiss it's a dif-

ferent story—and not only because they are naturally more cosmopolitan than the guys in New Jersey. They rotate jobs from country to country to help us learn each other's little ways, the company newsletters are full of contributions fed through from local markets, and conferences and seminars are a true two-way process. All this is because they know they depend on us out here for survival: the Swiss market is simply not big enough to recoup the terrifying research and development costs. In fact, most of my job relates to these circumstances: I am a sort of Janus figure, with one face turned toward Basel, explaining the South American scene in terms the HQ managers can understand, and the other face towards my Caribbean or Inca sales force, interpreting for them the thought processes of the alien Swiss and making them feel part of the family.

Let us leave the world of business for a while.

There is a clip of British War Office film from the early 1940s, showing a wing of Hurricanes lining up on a wave of German bombers somewhere over the North Sea. The soundtrack is synchronized from radio transmission, to give the full flavor of the event: you can actually hear what the men were saying to each other over the ether as they went in.

The men were Polish—all except the Flight Officer, who was as English as they come. He was concerned that the radio channel be kept clear for urgent warnings like "Look out, Johnny! Bandit on your tail!"

English Flight Officer: "Radio silence now. Good hunting."

You need a Polish interpreter to make sense of what follows: an explosion of bloodthirsty war-cries, boastful predictions of how many Jan is going to shoot down, bets being placed, and disrespectful comments about the long-haired English boy who seems to think he knows better than seasoned pilots how to go into action. Radio silence it is not.

Nevertheless, the British/Polish team did well in the Battle of Britain. Their objectives were clear, the enemy was visible, the crowds were cheering.

Under pressure like that, the barriers to international teamwork crumble—while the battle is on, at least.

All the issues are there in that airborne example. In some areas, circumstances made a plus for the team, in others a minus.

- **Issue 1: Motivation**
  All the fighter pilots shared the same goals: to knock down an enemy plane or two and return safe to base. Any individual who did not have these goals clearly in mind would soon find himself grounded. PLUS for team spirit.

- **Issue 2: Hierarchy**
  The "boss" was flying the same machine, facing the same dangers. The derision he faced from the rest of the team was conventional and healthy—not to be compared with the hatred servicemen under fire feel for the staff tucked safely away behind the lines, or on the ground. PLUS, on the whole.

- **Issue 3: Contact**
  The infantry lieutenant in the field can use his charisma (or his revolver) to maintain discipline. In his cockpit above the clouds, the Flight Officer was a bit cut off. MINUS for our flying team.

- **Issue 4: Culture**
  Eton is a long way from Warsaw. But the working cultures had a lot in common: a fighter pilot is a fighter pilot the world over. PLUS in the air, potential MINUS around the piano in the officers' mess.

- **Issue 5: Language**
  It is amusing to reflect that some of those Poles will have learnt "wizard prang" or "the magneto's knackered" (the jargon of the job) before they mastered the basics of English grammar. Certainly the ironic inflections of upper-class officers or Cockney ground crew will have meant little to them. MINUS overall for the team: the men doing the real job were largely cut off from their tactical decision maker, and from those providing the resources.

Having demonstrated how the five-issue analysis works, let us consider a more down-to-earth example, in the form of a short business case study.

Case Study

You are a Swede in the Stockholm head office of a company producing and marketing equipment for the world hospital market. Your company took over a big U.S. competitor two years ago, for market share to absorb the output of your new robotized plant in Germany. Your board decided to clean out the U.S. management team, but kept on the marketing director, Lou Salkin, now general manager of the U.S. subsidiary. You got your MBA three years ago, while Lou has just quit tennis because of arthritis.

Lou asks you to speak to his salespeople at their annual conference, because he has noticed that they persist in referring to the company and its products by the name of ACME—the company's name before the takeover. The salespeople, by the way, are making better money than they were before.

How will the encounter break down into the five categories?

Not such a nightmare as it seems at first glance:

- Very little *language* gap (if you are like any Swedish businessperson we have ever met);

- *Culture* is not too remote (some Americans might not quite know where Sweden is, but you have been watching American TV programs all your life)—but don't use too much of that MBA stuff in your presentation;

- Be direct on *hierarchy* (they will be on the lookout for signs of weakness);

- Seize this as a golden opportunity in terms of *contact,* and invite yourself to go out on the road with one of them for a day or two;

- Leave the issue of *motivation* to Lou—and that will motivate him. (You might suggest they hold their next annual conference on Swedish soil, if they hit their targets.)

Now what happens if we change the formula?

- Instead of the United States, set the scene in your Belgium/ Netherlands/ Luxembourg subsidiary. As a Swede, you are unlikely to be fluent in French, let alone Flemish. English is probably the best choice—but you will have to control it carefully: you are more accomplished in English than most Walloons (people living in Southern Belgium who speak French). And you will have to keep checking that you have really understood what the

Walloon is saying. *Language* problems will affect the result: it is difficult to transmit a subtle message with crude vocabulary, or through an interpreter.

• Instead of a flying visit, make it a two-year assignment: the nature of the *contact* changes. Now you have to make your tactical decisions, and shape your early messages, as a preparation for a set of relationships, rather than aiming simply for initial impact.

• You are a junior staff person from HQ addressing the local board: issues of *hierarchy* become more delicate.

• Your audience is drawn from both sides of the Belgian Flemish-Walloon divide, with some real Dutch and Luxembourgeois thrown in: you are no longer on a level playing field in terms of *culture*. Should you try to cater for the internal tensions?

• And finally, you have personal doubts about the message you have been asked to deliver. Perhaps the subsidiary would be better off going its own sweet way without interference. What happens to your *motivation*, and how well placed are you to motivate others?

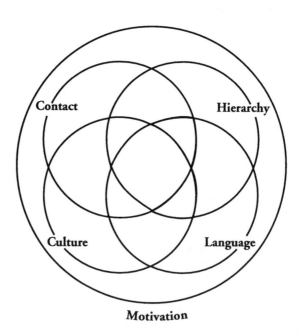

Motivation

In the diagram above, motivation embraces all the other circles. This can be interpreted in two ways:

- That mutual motivation between the head office type and his or her counterpart in the foreign subsidiary can only flourish when the other four factors have been put in order and are running smoothly;

- That somebody somewhere had better find the motivation to make sure that the other four factors *are* put in order and *do* run smoothly. (This is typically the job of the human resources specialist. The role of human resources changes dramatically once a company goes international.

We will now build that diagram, circle by circle, paying particular attention to the areas where the circles overlap.

Language

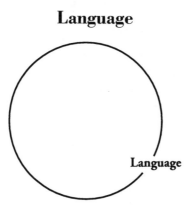

Language

Let us consider an international conference, within a multinational company.

The delegates seated around the table are national representatives from Italy, France, Brazil, Venezuela, Germany, the United States, Singapore, Japan, the United Kingdom, Sweden… The language in use will certainly be English.

Now the question: of those listed, who has the trickiest problem as a communicator?

Answer: the American and the Briton, probably.

So long as the conversation is limited to practical business matters, there will be an unspoken agreement among the others to conduct the meeting in a simplified, general-purpose version of English. In its fully-fledged idiomatic form, English is notoriously difficult to handle, and most non-native speakers settle for a rudimentary version: a tool to get the job done.

An insider, who has grown up speaking some version of "real" English without thinking, finds it difficult to step down from this lofty perch and make each point with simplified syntax, controlled idiom and vocabulary. When a native speaker does try to make adjustments, the result is usually clumsy and ineffectual—embarrassed and embarrassing, in fact.

Here is a true story to illustrate the need.

Civil aircraft manufacturers run highly sophisticated sales operations, which place great emphasis on good client relations. After all, there are only so many airlines in the world to buy the machines they make. One manufacturer we know well employs several nationalities in its sales/technical support functions, and English is the company language—both inside, and in communication with most of its customers.

Recently, a South-East Asian client introduced a new condition for future dealings: they were happy to communicate in English, as all their key employees were competent, but would the manufacturer please ensure that from now on no native speakers of English were involved? They were too hard to understand, and apparently had difficulty in understanding what was said to them...

Chapter 6 is largely devoted to describing this phenomenon, and suggesting practical ways around it. We have called the language for international use "*Overseas English*".

Culture

Culture was our concern in Chapter 1.

We hope that you already see the value of *facts/attitudes/behavior* model building as a more coherent approach than the random accumulation of cross-cultural tips and hints.

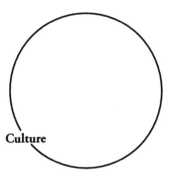

Culture

Our corporate seagull must also pay attention to the attitudes that go with given functions in a corporation. When we have written case studies for management trainees, we have often sought a universal conflict which they would all recognize. To make the case study lively, the trick is to exaggerate the conflict: salespeople on the road think that marketing people have their heads in the clouds and are detached from reality; both groups suspect the production manager of obstructiveness, while the production manager thinks they only exist to disrupt carefully-laid production plans; the financial controller believes that the company exists to balance its books, and is seen by everybody else as a secret policeman; the training manager in HRD has the company's future in the palm of his or her hand, but has great difficulty seducing people away from their desks to attend vital training courses.

Of course, in a well-ordered company, such clashes of interest should be a thing of the past, but when you are an outsider on a visit, it is wise to assume that they are still there. People love to form armed camps. Never plan on the basis that the people in the subsidiary are all one happy family, even if they try to give you that impression.

The way a culture speaks

We were present recently at a strategy planning session in Eastern Europe. The event was to be spread over a weekend, and conducted in English and Hungarian simultaneously—through a relaxed system of interpreting that would ensure nobody felt left out.

The first job to be done—and it was taken very seriously—was to reach agreement on the form of address appropriate to the weekend. First-name familiarity was natural to the Americans and British present,

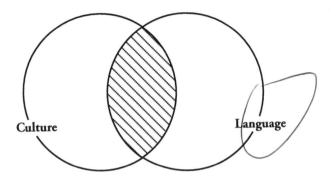

whose average age was in the early thirties. The Hungarian contingent included several rather older members, who seemed likely to stand on their dignity. The chairman addressed them first, and asked their permission for first names and familiar grammar (*te* rather than *ön*— a subtlety that does not occur in English, since the death of the *thou/you* distinction). This was not just a formality: the older generation consulted each other with raised eyebrows and agreed with nods. "Good," sighed the chairman, "it is done."

Soon afterwards, one of the Hungarians expressed regret that "cliques" had been forming in the offices. The Americans shrugged it off—it always happens, and who cares anyway? The Hungarians closed ranks: *they* cared. A lot of fuss about nothing? We asked the two groups to give us their associations around the word "clique". The Americans offered "tennis, parties, fun, gossip" and the Hungarians "conspiracy, power-seeking, wickedness, dictatorship".

Look for associations and connotations. Do not trust the first definition you find in a dictionary.

> We dissect nature along lines laid down by our native languages.
> Benjamin Lee Whorf, linguist

Language is not only what you speak in. Much deeper than that, it is what you think with—you cannot think about something you cannot name.

The way a culture thinks

Here we touch on a difference in patterns of thought and styles of argument which we have often seen create tension. When a representative of Culture A tells a Culture B partner "You are not being logical", the meaning usually is "You are approaching this issue in an unfamiliar, disturbing way".

The form of reasoning instilled in Northern European and American school children goes like this: examine all the evidence, try to detect a pattern, form a general rule to cover all cases, subject your newly-formed rule to rigorous testing. If it survives, you have your theory, policy or proposal. If not, you have learned a great deal during the process. So a good teacher spends a long time exercising pupils' minds *before* giving them the answer. In subjects like literature and history, there is often no answer.

In Southern Europe, and in Catholic enclaves further north, educational systems are often still redolent of the catechism: "Who made the world?" "God made the world"—and everything follows from that. The seventeenth-century philosopher Descartes started his approach to the truth by clearing his mind of all but one undeniable statement: "I think, therefore I am." On that he built his system. Descartes is still a powerful influence on the French way of thinking.

> Much of the best and worst in the French national spirit can be imputed to this concept of education as inspired academic pedagogy confined to the classroom walls: its role is to transmit knowledge and to train intellects, not...to develop the full individual.
>
> John Ardagh, *France in the 1980s*

Two sets of factors emerge:

A	B
Northern Europe/United States	Southern Europe
Protestant	Catholic
Germanic/Anglo-Saxon	Latin
Education = Development	Education = Instruction
Loose school curricula	Centralized curriculum
Experience has value	Qualifications have value

A person from a background scoring five out of six in Column A is likely to approach any given problem differently from a Column B type.

So when John Stevens tries to persuade Jean-Marie Dupont to his point of view, all his background culture is pushing him to begin from the basic known facts and work up: "As you know, 80 percent of our customers are regular buyers. We've got an 11 percent market share. Inflation is dropping. And there are several other factors we should consider before we start to explore the various avenues that are open to us...."

Jean-Marie has his teeth clenched. He wants to hear John's proposal up front, so that they can do as he was taught at school, and seek evidence in support of that proposal. He feels that the man from headquarters is patronizing him by stating the obvious, and exhibits his natural impatience: "Yes, yes. I see all that, of course! The best approach is obviously to..."

"So irrational, so impatient, so Latin!" thinks John.

"So pedestrian, so cold, so American", thinks Jean-Marie.

To sum up:

- Column A cultures tend to present like this: "The facts are;...and these are the most relevant facts;...so we can see various ways forward..., of which *this* is the best..."

- Column B cultures tend to present arguments as follows: "*This* is the best way forward because...and because...and because...and here are some more underlying facts..."

Hierarchy

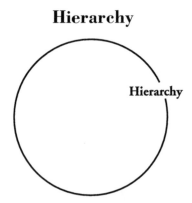

Hierarchy

For our corporate seagull, the important thing to remember is that there are mutually antagonistic mind-sets in head office and in the subsidiary. The subsidiary perceives HQ as bureaucratic, academic, and overstaffed with patricians reclining on couches eating grapes. Meanwhile HQ views the subsidiary as shortsighted, ignorant of the broad view, suspicious of new initiatives and prone to making promises they have no intention of keeping.

We bring these tensions to the surface on management training courses with a simple jigsaw puzzle. Two teams are told that they are managers (M) and workers (W) respectively. The M team are told to brief the W team to assemble the pieces of the puzzle.

They immediately assume that the W team will not be bright enough to work it out for themselves, and spend an inordinate amount of time planning, drafting step-by-step instructions, and guarding the door of the M room against intrusion. The W team spends a corresponding period waiting for information, building up resentment, and probably planning a strike. The referees have to be alert: longstanding relationships can be damaged when a W realizes that an old friend only has to become an M in order to treat all Ws like fools.

We have found this hierarchical stereotype to be even stronger than ethnic or geographical distinctions. All acts of communication along the spokes of the wheel take place against this background of suspicion.

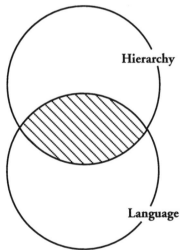

Here is a tip for John (from HQ), when he has an idea to get across to Jean-Marie (subsidiary). Don't say "*We* think you can tighten your belts in the third quarter of the financial year", say rather "*I* think you can etc, etc". If the manager from the subsidiary hears that "we" form, he or she perceives a *fait accompli* imposed by a faceless gang who have little idea of what it means to make a living in the real world. The manager might even suspect that you personally have doubts about the validity of the statement. Using "I" leaves the way open for true person-to-person dealing, and reserves the "we" to represent John plus Jean-Marie—the team who will solve the problem together.

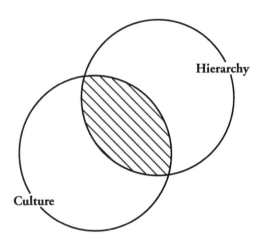

The official organization chart in your subsidiary probably reflects the corporate view on how things should be run. It does not necessarily match the feelings of the people on the ground. Those feelings grow, in large measure, out of the local country culture.

How likely is that culture to see a command structure as an inverted pyramid, with the bosses supporting the people who are doing the real work?

On some organigrams today, we find top management in the left-hand margin, with salaries decreasing as we read from left to right—a compromise, perhaps, but an indication that the company is not run on strictly top-down principles.

The seagull has to modify his or her style when the laws of gravity are changed.

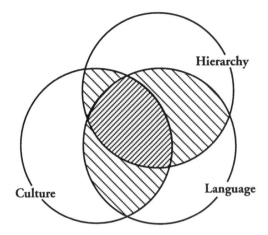

Here is a true story to sum this up, and again it involves John and Jean-Marie:

The Frenchman had been working for the Americans for three years, and it was a good deal: he was running one of their French subsidiaries, hitting his targets, getting on well with his staff, using his local knowledge to effect improvements in distribution. Yet he didn't feel trusted, somehow, by HQ in Boston. They always looked at him a little critically during meetings. He took it up with John.

"Tell me, Jean-Marie—yes, I will have a little more wine—when was the last time you had this feeling?"

"Well, for example, at this year's budget conference in January. It all went smoothly for a day-and-a-half, there seemed to be a general meeting of minds. And yet..."

"What actually happened? Who said what?"

"The chairman asked me formally if I was prepared to commit myself to this very tough budget."

"And what did you say?"

"Well naturally I said 'Why not?'" (Accompanying this with an enormous Gallic shrug...)

When an American asks you earnestly to commit yourself to an earnest business proposition, he or she wants a level gaze, and no hint of irony or light-heartedness. When a Frenchman is asked if he can take a machine-gun nest single-handed, his self-image demands that he deliver that existential shrug, stub out an imaginary Gauloise, and go over the top with a grin.

Contact

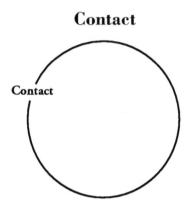

In our original ideal picture at the beginning of this section (cozy team-work with no complicating factors), you had plenty of opportunity for informal contact with that colleague in the same office.

If your partner is a long way away you have to *plan* for contact. We have collected tips from experienced international managers on how to do this planning. Here are a few of our favorites:

- I try to visit each of my subsidiaries four times a year:
  —budget;
  —budget review;
  —let's clear the desk of paperwork and talk blue skies;
  —I understand the salmon fishing is good at this time of year.
  General manager, toiletries firm

- Whether the visit is four hours or three days, I always devote the first 51 percent of the agenda to local problems. I listen, offer sympathy and advice if appropriate. Then and only then do I start talking about corporate objectives and the local contri-bution. The managers down there are in no mood to listen to what I have to say until they've got their worries off their chests.
  Senior partner, international consultancy group

- Even when you think they've got the idea, put in a call a few days after you've left, just to check. Find a pretext—"I've lost my notes of the meeting" will do—and ask them to give their version of what was agreed. You'll be amazed at the distortions that can creep in.

  Desk manager for Western Europe, American
  light engineering group

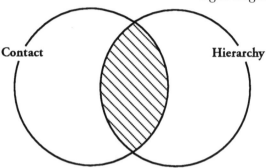

There is a delicate balance to be struck between taking an interest in what subordinates are doing, and breathing down their necks. Nothing is more demotivating than to have the boss, on a flying visit, tampering with systems you have developed and which produce excellent results.

Picture a kitchen where one partner is cooking, from instinct and years of practice, a dish that has never failed to please. The other appears with a cookery book open at the relevant page and begins to offer constructive criticism...

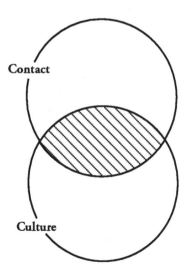

There is a close correspondence between the subordinate's tolerance of interference and a sense of personal space.

In cultures where men walk arm-in-arm along the street, there is a greater readiness to accept guidance at close quarters—provided it is delivered with due regard for all the other factors in the relationship.

In regions where people seldom touch more closely than an arm's-length handshake, it is better not to interfere unless invited.

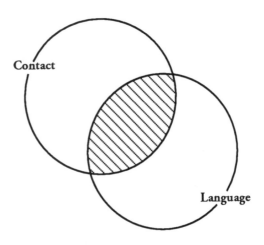

I have a million ideas and only five hundred English words.
                                    Senior engineer, Italian tire company

If your command of English-as-lingua-franca is good, please be considerate of those who are only just surviving. We have seen stress build up to the point of tears in strong businesspeople who have been forced to sit through four-hour meetings, concentrating not only on the business at hand, but on following the language and formulating their ideas fast enough to contribute.

Call frequent breaks for their sake. In terms of the quality of information exchanged and ideas generated, it will be more efficient than just going on and on.

If, on the other hand, you are the sufferer, don't be afraid to ask for a short break—perhaps to discuss the last agenda point with colleagues in your own language, to make sure you have things clear.

A Final Anecdote

Getting things clear was Lars Svensson's job. Equipped with his MBA, he was dispatched by headquarters in Sweden to tour the subsidiaries, meet the people, and gather data for the new five-year sales plan in the power generation division. The French subsidiary, recently acquired, was operating a policy of disinformation. The chief executive officer felt that the best way to preserve autonomy was to keep HQ in the dark. The figure he gave to Lars was deliberately distorted.

The British manager felt it would be unkind to deliver her usual line on forecasts ("We're not selling knives and forks! How can you have a forecast for power stations?"). Instead, she took Lars for a long lunch, gossiped for a while about HQ politics, and gave him a gently pessimistic figure to put in his briefcase.

The Italian explained how different things always are in Italy—fragmented market, everything depending on a network of contacts, how the time he was spending with Lars would have been better spent cultivating those contacts…and gave him a random figure to play with.

The German provided a ring-bound volume full of calculations, based on interlocking best-case/worst-case analyses, predictions of D-Mark fluctuations, and statistical breakdowns of the competition's performance over the last 20 years.

The American leaned over the table, bared his teeth, and said: "My forecast? I'll give you my forecast…. We're gonna win!"

Lars returned to HQ, entered all the data he had collected in his personal computer, and produced a curve.

He gave it to the chief executive officer, who hung it on his office wall.

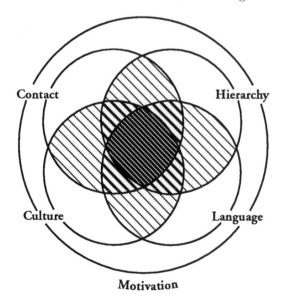

Contact   Hierarchy

Culture   Language

Motivation

The Cultures of Gangsterism

The 1989 thriller *Black Rain* portrayed the misadvantures of an American cop taking on Japanese mobsters (*yakuza*) on their home territory. The bullets do the same job, but the triggers are pulled for different reasons. Our hero needs a local cop to help him understand the motivations of the criminals.

> The *yakuza* gives Japan's no-hopers a role, a uniform, a lapel badge, a company song, an in-house magazine, and a relationship of childlike dependency to the Boss. It gives them, in Japanese terms, a life. For what is life without these things?
>
> *The Independent,*
> 3 February 1990

A British release, *The Krays,* shows an American criminal bigshot paying a business visit to his London counterparts, the Krays, whose welcome gift to him is a photograph of themselves with their loving family—a recognition on their part of the "family" nature of organized crime in America.

Another film, *The Long Good Friday* details the clash between a London gangster and the IRA, who are moving in on his territory. Their hard-bitten ideological motivations puzzle him; trying to deal with them according to his own "ethics" gets him into deadly trouble.

In *The Godfather,* the chief adviser to generations of *mafiosi* is an Irish American, who acts as a bridge between the criminals and the Irish-dominated New York police department.

The criminal gangs of Moscow overlap with the local "hooligans" and black marketeers, whose style and livelihood revolve around the scarce supply of fashionable Western goods.

The drug barons of Colombia and the Golden Triangle of South-East Asia rule in a style that local guerrilla leaders or warlords would recognize, and police methods for dealing with them are adapted accordingly.

The pickpocket gangs who roam Europe's shopping streets and sporting events are indistinguishable at airports from the tourists they prey on.

Next time you relax with a thriller, try to add something to your working model of the world's business cultures.

CHAPTER THREE

Character

Your business partners are more than their company's delegate or mouthpiece. They are a human being, with standards, drives and moods. The human relationship is crucial to good business.

Ten lands are more easily known than one man.

Yiddish proverb

At the end of Chapter 1, we encouraged you to start developing a flexible model of the culture from which your business partner springs. We also pointed out the need to be alert to deviations from the norms that make up your model. The deviations you encounter will often be an expression of individual character traits; it is important not to let your expectations of, say, Chinese behavior blind you to the behavior patterns of the particular Chinese you are dealing with.

It is this individual character who should be hearing your message, buying your product, supporting you in the team. You can only improve your chances if you take steps to shape your arguments to appeal to this individual—your partner. Where is he starting from? Where is he going? What does she know? What does she want?

We are all deeply aware of social taboos, including the rule against probing too deeply into others' feelings. And when we are among strangers, it is particularly easy to get things wrong.

> I started conversation with the men opposite [on a train in China]…They turned out to be professional painters and administrators in an art museum, but when I asked one about his feelings for landscape, I realised that I'd gone too far. His gaze detached itself, his smile expanded, and he said nothing. But the official beside him looked appalled, and whispered across to me: "Mr. Kung is now Deputy Director of our museum. You cannot ask such personal things"…
>
> Colin Thubron, *Behind the Wall*

On the other hand:

> I was at a reception during my first business trip to China, and making conversation with a member of the host delegation. I don't know why, but I suddenly wanted to know something about him personally. It spilled out: "What happened to you during the Cultural Revolution?"
>
> He became very excited, called for everybody's attention, and made an announcement in Mandarin, very heated, gesturing to-

wards me. I could see from his colleagues' reaction that they were shocked, and I wanted the ground to open up and swallow me. They gathered in a huddle, gesticulating earnestly and ignoring me completely.

I turned in despair to a more experienced colleague, who understood Mandarin. He was very reassuring: "Disaster? Quite the opposite. They might never have found a way of raising the subject among themselves, although the Cultural Revolution was the biggest event by far in so many lives. Now they're having a real conversation about it, and all thanks to you."

French civil engineer

This was more by luck than judgment, of course. But if you take no risks in this area, you have no chance at all of getting lucky.

Try looking at it this way: being a stranger to local customs means either walking in fear of getting things wrong, and so doing nothing, or using your forgivable ignorance as a license to dig a bit deeper.

In this chapter we will be suggesting how to do that digging.

Our suggestions are chiefly in the form of questions. As your working relationship with a given partner develops, these are some of the questions to which you should be finding answers.

Is There Some Deep General Principle My Partner Is Applying?

Business is business the world over, of course, But often there is some other strong drive behind your partner—a more or less atavistic force that he or she might hardly be conscious of. The force could derive from the local background culture, or else from the principles of the organization employer. (Many companies these days have enshrined values: "Dedication; Teamwork; Decisiveness; Excellence.")

A good way to start exploring Character is by testing responses to proverbs. We often use the following short questionnaire as the starting point for a discussion on this theme.

Try it on yourself. Then turn to some results we obtained from a variety of nationalities.

Proverbs Questionnaire

Look at the following proverbs and sayings. How central are the points they make to the way you run your life, both business and personal? Give a mark on the scale from 0 = Irrelevant, to 8 = Essential.

"Time is money"
0   1   2   3   4   5   6   7   8

"Blood is thicker than water"
0   1   2   3   4   5   6   7   8

"My word is my bond"
0   1   2   3   4   5   6   7   8

"God will provide"
0   1   2   3   4   5   6   7   8

"Do as you would be done by"
0   1   2   3   4   5   6   7   8

Commentary

The graphs show average results from a handful of cultures: Japanese, Arab, French, Italian, Spanish, German, Swiss and British. The sample sizes were in the dozens, the respondents were all middle and senior managers involved in international business.

Individual responses can never be predicted, but some significant patterns emerge within each culture.

Time is money

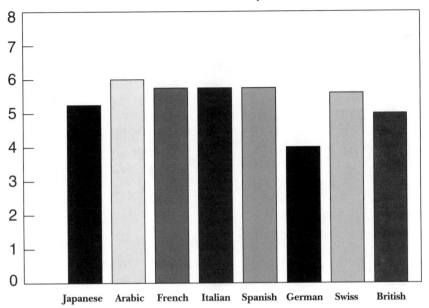

Our panel members often found themselves splitting their business view of time from their private view. Some of the scores represent an arithmetical compromise between the two.

Non-German readers might have expected Germans to endorse the time-is-money principle. A generation ago that might have been the case. Nowadays, the view tends to be: Time at work should be carefully managed in order to maximize free time.

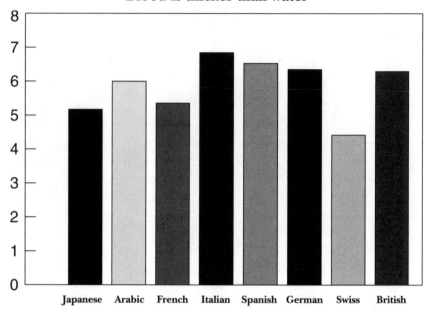

Discussion of this proverb centers on making sacrifices for the family in the interests of career and company, and also on the question of nepotism.

The Arab response is perhaps surprising: the Arab way of life puts great emphasis on family, and Arab businesses are often run on family lines. But our Arab respondents are not traditional Arab merchants; they are executives working for multinational companies (mainly in Egypt and other Eastern Mediterranean countries).

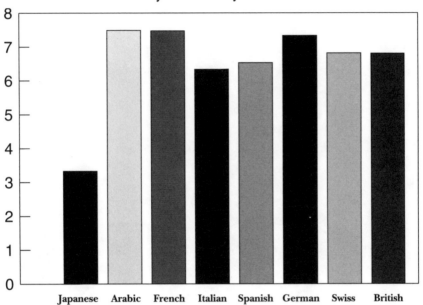

My word is my bond

Almost all respondents value their personal reputation under this heading. Where they give a score of less than 8, they refer to the need to temper the ideal with realism.

The Japanese reaction should be seen in relation to their pragmatic, exploratory approach and to their feeling for the group. What is truth, if it disturbs the harmony?

God will provide

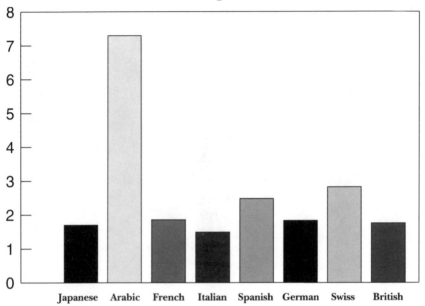

Most respondents took this in a religious sense, referring to a pesronal deity. Some understood it as a more general reference to the degree of push required to achieve things in life.

On this point, the Arab panel (which includes some Christians), gives a response which accords with most outsiders' expectations. Japan, in spite of frequent images in the western media of temples and meditating monks, is a highly secular society.

Do as you would be done by

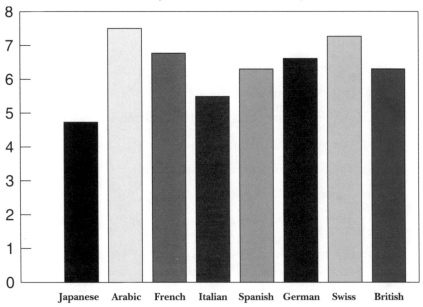

This proverb is close to the New Testament sentiment "Love thy neighbor". Most discussions were about fair play, and whether it helped the fair player in the long run. Some respondents, including a surprising number of native English speakers, misread the grammar of the sentence and take it to mean "Do as you have been done by", closer to the Old Testament principle of "An eye for an eye". This introduces some distortion into the results.

What Kind of Childhood Did My Partner Have?

Of course, if you spring that question on a business partner in the back of a taxi, he or she might flinch a little. Nevertheless:

> Give us the child before the age of seven and it will be ours for life.
> Jesuit educational principle

Here is a questionnaire that explores the formative years. Try it yourself. Try it on a friend, on a colleague, on your neighbor on a long-distance flight. Draw on it for inspiration when you are on business in another country and small talk starts to run thin.

- What's your first memory?

- How close was your family?

- Who was your first friend outside the family?

- What are your first memories of formal education?

- What made you happy/unhappy as a child?

- What was your first ambition?

- What were the first external forces you were conscious of?

We ran this questionnaire with people from five nations: Poland, Scotland, Sweden, Tunisia and Zaire. Here we set you a puzzle.

Which is the Polish response to the first question? It might help you to know that the Pole we interviewed is now a Canadian, 73 years old and semi-retired. He is still on the board of several manufacturing companies, and an adviser to Polish industry...

What's your first memory?

- I'm looking down through the banisters at a lady in a fur cape. She's coming up *the winding stairway* out of the darkness at the bottom. The angle makes it all foreshortened, she's looking up. A smell of mothballs, alien. Perhaps I was two.

- I was two or three when I first went to *the nursery school* in the village where I was born. But the memory is hazy compared to that of my first day at primary school—like the difference between hearing a symphony on an old mono record, and then from a full orchestra in a great concert hall.

- I remember being carried, *on my mother's back* or on my father's shoulders, the rhythm, the feeling of warmth and closeness...

- "Can you really read?" said my mother, pleasantly surprised. I remember clearly, sitting with my mother picking *words out of the newspaper.* It seemed to have come naturally to me; my mother hadn't put any special effort into it, and neither had I.

- My first memory is of starting school, sitting on a bench with a slate in one hand and a *piece of chalk* in the other, learning the letters. I was young, just four years old. My father was the maths teacher, and he arranged for me to start earlier than normal.

We expect you are finding it difficult to find the Pole. He is the one who went to the nursery school. No strong clues so far in the pocket autobiography. The rest of his responses to the questionnaire, and those of the other four participants, are below.

Commentary

The Polish Canadian, remember, was "the nursery school". Here are his responses to the rest of the childhood questionnaire.

Family feelings were subdued, but strong. My brother would always stand up for me in a fight, but we never showed much emotion. My mother was warm, but my father set himself up as a tough model: "I made it, so you'd better do the same" was his line… "If you get beaten, it means you let it happen". Living on a farm brings out character very early.

My first friend was the boy next door. He was a year older than me…

…so when he was due to start primary school, I was still too young. I kicked up a hell of a row, crying and complaining, until the teacher accepted me. But I was always a slow starter: when he passed the exams to the secondary school and I didn't, I felt pretty frustrated. But he was very naughty and eventually his bad behavior held him back. I caught up in the long run.

I loved horse-riding, preferably bare-back. That gave me a feeling of manhood. If somebody put me down, or had visible proof that he was better than me, that brought out my competitive streak: "I can beat them".

I was good at things: music or sport or fighting…this urge to prove myself turned into intellectual ambition, a feeling of responsibility for myself and for others.

The stratified society. Some people were worse off than us, some better. That struck me from a very early age and got me thinking—not envy (my mother made me grateful for what we had), just aware of the differences. My politics, tending to the left, stem from that.

There were four other interviewees. Here are their answers to the other six questions on the list.

"The winding stairway" was the Scot—a 43-year–old woman, now commercial artist.

> I was the only child in a one-parent, two-grandparent household. Often sent to stay with various aunts and uncles. That made me feel privileged. Like a VIP. Family entertainments were always fun—songs, recitations and laughter.
>
> My first playmate was a little blond boy, child of a friend of my mother's. I was expected to enjoy his company simply because he was my age. I found him unbearably dull. It wasn't till I was about eight that I really started to enjoy being with children my own age.
>
> On the way to school for the first time, I wept at visions of years of boredom, studying dull maps. On arrival I was disgusted to find some of the other children couldn't tie their shoe-laces. But what delight to find that the teacher was marvellous and lessons were going to be fun. By the end of the first morning, I had thrown my arms round her thighs and said "I love you!"
>
> I was happiest scrambling over sea-rocks on days so wet and windy that only other noble spirits would go out. Misery was being tormented and jeered at by other kids, especially during school lunches. We had to eat every scrap but I couldn't stomach the mutton fat. They always caught me trying to spit it into my handkerchief.
>
> My first ambition was to do a handstand dive off the 10-metre board. I managed it with surprising ease and have had no clear ambition since.
>
> The Cuban crisis was the first I remember hearing about, but it was the Kennedy assassination that first touched me. I wept in empathy with the crowds on the cinema screen.

"On my mother's back" was the Zairois—40 years old and a professor of information science working in a British university:

> It was a very close family indeed.
>
> An old woman, a neighbour, was my first friend. She used to bring me milk and sing me songs…
>
> Those were my pleasures: songs and talking to elderly people and walking long distances through the countryside. What I hated was hav-

ing my sleep disturbed on a Sunday morning to go to church. My mother was always very strict about religious observance and we kids resented it; but we've since become even more religious than she is.

Going to school was like magic—I was amazed that the teachers could get us to know things that we didn't know before. School was so marvellous that I even wanted to carry on at the weekend.

I admired and imitated these teacher-magicians and wanted to become one.

The outside world first appeared in the form of a Chaplin film, full of flowers and laughter. But I also remember war, seeing soldiers in action all around our house.

"Words out of the newspaper" was the Swede: 35, an engineer in the electrical industry, and mother of a growing family ("a typical Swedish working mother with split ambitions between work and family").

It was a very strongly united family. I was raised on a farm, which my mother and father loved. They worked incredibly hard and were never away. Our whole life was there.

That farm was fairly isolated, so we didn't have much contact with neighbours. My first friend was a girl at school, when I was seven. We shared secrets and jokes.

I remember standing in line at the school gate, thrilled at being in a new place and the prospect of doing something on my own. My elder sister argued at great length with my father to let me go to school one year earlier than normal.

The best thing was being with animals on the farm. Playing with dogs, horses, calves. My father playing with me on the kitchen floor—my parents didn't have much time to spare for us, so when they did it felt very special. And going to town to buy new clothes—a rare treat. When an animal got hurt, especially if someone hurt it intentionally—that upset me greatly, and still does. But there was not much unhappiness.

I always wanted to do everything, to learn everything—history, psychology, technology. The most difficult thing was to choose.

The murder of President Kennedy. We heard the news on the radio and the family discussed it. Terrible, unexpected, remote.

"A piece of chalk" was the Tunisian. At 42, he is a pharmacist, and trains the sales team in a U.S. multinational.

We were seven brothers and two sisters, and family life was all-embracing. That had its positive and negative sides. Father was very strict with us.

Once when I was about six, during an afternoon nap I wet the bed. My father went to the kitchen, heated a knife and touched it against my leg. I woke up yelling. At the same moment there were two doctors at the door. Father had called them in advance. I never wet the bed again and I still have a little mark on my leg. But the atmosphere was warm and secure: I learned to compete and to support. Everything you need for family life as an adult.

My first friend is still my friend. I met him in the second year of school. We had interests in common but opposite temperaments. He was calm, while I was more playful and quick to anger. I felt good with him because he could accept my aggressiveness. I've learned to control it now, but he probably helped that. That contrast is still there—he's a rather serious fellow, running his own business; I'm more out-going with a bit of a wild streak still.

My greatest triumph as a child was when I passed my first exam. It was such a priority in my family.

Frustration was when my parents didn't take me seriously. That led to tears. I couldn't fight my father, so I had to use woman's weapons. I always wanted to win, a poor loser.

Photos of planes made me dream of becoming a pilot.

A union leader was shot by the colonial powers just near our house. He was a fine man and a friend of my father's. That event awoke my political passions.

How Normal a Product of His Cultural Background Is My Partner? And How Typical of His Company?

Having developed your model of your partner's way of life, and having studied the values of his or her organization, you now have a reference point against which to measure your partner:

- My partner seems to be a stickler for detail, but is he exceptionally so, given his background?

- My partner avoids committing herself on paper whenever she can. Is this unusual?

- My partner never stops singing his company's praises. Is he just part of the chorus?

What Self-Contradictions Is My Partner Trying to Resolve?

The Swiss psychologist Jung suggested that beneath the level of daily thoughts, each unconscious mind is striving to resolve and balance countervailing forces—light/dark, masculine/feminine... It is the contradictions and tensions within a person that catch our attention; without them, there would be no material for psychological biographies.

> Do I contradict myself?
> Very well then I contradict myself,
> (I am large, I contain multitudes).
> Walt Whitman

Jung was also the creator of the idea of introvert and extrovert. The terminology has entered popular awareness, but it is worth remembering that there is more to this than "extrovert = jolly", "introvert = shy". It is quite possible to be a shy extrovert or a placidly confident introvert, as a moment's study of this ready-reckoner will reveal:

Introvert	*Extrovert*
Achievement	Status
Fulfillment	Respect
Task	People
Knowledge	Action
Understanding	Domination
Inward	Outward
Fantasy	Fact

So the supplementary questions you might find yourself asking include:

- Is this dynamic individual just desperate for my respect?

- Is this quiet individual about to roll over me on his or her way to personal fulfillment?

Is My Partner's Personality Integrated With the Organization, or Is He or She Wearing a Mask?

Being employed in a corporation is a recent phenomenon—it's hardly natural at all. When we enter employment, we accept that our behavior will be modified. The rules vary from job to job, employer to employer. The copywriter in the creative department of an advertising agency has greater latitude, traditionally, than the teller in a bank, while the farmhand can be freer than either.

A farmhand who suddenly discovered a talent for advertising slogans would have a hard time adjusting to the pace of life of Madison Avenue. If he survived for long enough, though, the demands on his behavior would begin to affect his attitude.

We can show it diagrammatically like this:

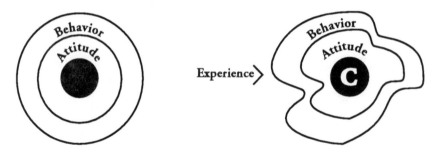

As the outer circle (Behavior) is pushed and pulled into the shape a career requires, so the circle within (Attitude) flexes accordingly. If your job requires you to get up at 5:00 AM—a change in behavior—your attitude to bed changes too. If your attitude to your company's products is blocking your success as a salesperson, you work on it, and the improvement shines through in your behavior.

And the fixed ring in the middle? The one that does not change shape? Character.

In society at large, and in the workplace in particular, there are limits to how far Tom can make changes in Harry, how deeply he can cut with his criticism. These limits are not always clearly defined, but crossing them is always deeply resented.

"Criticize what I *do*, but never what I *am*."

The size of the Character circle in our diagram is arbitrary. Should it dominate the picture, suggesting that the Self is very powerful, wearing a veneer in the workplace? Or should it be a mere dot, suggesting that the Self is deeply hidden while its owner gets on with the vital jobs of earning a living, building a career, and generally fitting in?

Often, as people follow their career paths, they become more personally involved in their work. More and more they are what they do.

Of course, there are local variations:

> I have noticed that many of my British colleagues use what the Japanese call *tatemae,* or outside face. In general, the British tend to be more formal or diplomatic, while Americans tend to be more direct, emotive and explosive, showing the real face, or *honne.*
>
> An American management trainer working for a British company in Tokyo

How Is My Partner Viewed by Colleagues, or by the Boss?

Make a deliberate effort to watch how your partner's team functions within itself. What is the pecking order? Where does he or she stand in it? How do colleagues react when your partner makes a proposal? How formally do they address him or her?

Is your partner feared? Respected? Tolerated? Despised?

> There are four types of young officer. The stupid and lazy ones you can forget about: either the enemy or their own men will dispose of them. The intelligent and lazy will stay out of harm's way: pay them no attention. Then we have the intelligent, energetic type: beware, they want your position. Finally, there are the stupid, energetic ones: it is your job to take them out and shoot them before they ruin everything.
>
> attributed to the Duke of Wellington

What Sort of Mood Is My Partner In? How Is His or Her Mind Working?

As behavioral psychology has broadened and diversified, new tools have emerged.

Neuro Linguistic Programming (NLP) is such a tool. Put very simply, it divides mental activity into three types: visual, auditory and kinaesthetic.

Each person functions predominantly in one of these modes, switching to the others occasionally. *Eye movements* and *choice of idiom* provide the clues.

Eye Movements

The visual mode can be identified by eye movements in the upward direction, the auditory by horizontal and the kinaesthetic by downward glances.

Choice of Idiom

I *see*...let's focus on...look into it...shed some light...ray of hope...light at the end of the tunnel...

Sounds good to me...I hear you...listen...I'd echo that...fine-tuning...not much to shout about...I wouldn't say that...let's say

My *feeling* is...I go along with you there...we hit it off well...keep in touch...kick this idea around...can't put my finger on it.

NLP helps to make the vital step from "What sort of mood is my partner in?" to "Is there an adjustment I can make so as to harmonize more effectively?"

Which of My Many Arguments Should I Mobilize for This Partner?

We took a group of seven people: all compatriots, all in their 30s, all doing the same job for the same firm. We told them: "Please will you each take a piece of paper and write, on one side only, your thoughts about that piece of paper. No further instructions."

Here are the results:

	MATERIALS	CONTENT FORM	MOOD
Flip chart 2A — yyway-who es-<u>now</u> get _going_ pity it's not red	Pencil; green and orange felt-tip	"This paper & pen suit me."	Exuberant
Teddy bear stationery	Pencil	Technical; Job in printing company	Descriptive; reminiscent
Quality A4	Fountain pen	"I am your paper speaking."	Bitter
Yellow flimsy	Ball point	Free association	Sensual
Lined	Fibre tip	Mind gap	Explorative
Torn loose-leaf	Red felt-tip	Four line rhyme	Oracular
10 x 10 cm.	Pencil	Epigram on lost potential	Sad

The diversity is striking. It would be a great mistake to assume that other people's ways of thinking parallel your own.

Woman (strikingly dressed, and clearly no slave to fashion): "I'm interested in those shoes in the front of the window."
Shoe salesman: "Oh, yes, they're very popular this season; we're selling a lot of them."
Husband: "That's no way to sell to this lady."

The salesman should have read the signals, and adapted his message to the individual. Here is an exercise to help you explore that principle.

There is a boat. Your job is to sell it. It is a high class boat with the following excellent features:

- fast, reliable, economical, clean, quiet engine

- radio

- navigation gear

- sail

- lines

- previous owners

- guest berths

- showers

- bar

- racing history.

Up comes a man in his 60s—well dressed, a bit too well fed, with a confident bearing. Retired banker, perhaps? Which features would you emphasize as you describe the boat to him?

Now a young woman—fit, tanned, wearing an expensive sports chronometer that she glances at as she approaches. Tailor your sales pitch to fit her.

Next a company director in his early 40s. His business card shows that the company bears his name. Is it an old family firm, or did he build it up himself? If you could get the answer to that question, how would it affect the way you promoted the boat to him? And if his two teenage sons appeared halfway through the conversation?

So far we have presented you with potential customers identified by simple, crude labels. Think for a moment now about what you would say if your father came down the gangway, or your boss, or your accountant? Even better, think of three people you know well who are superficially in the same category: three department heads from your company, say, or three suppliers from whom you buy. Think of their individual traits and how you would appeal to them by high-lighting features of the boat.

This approach is, of course, built into "How to Sell" courses and the thinking of every advertising man or lawyer. Much of the second half of this book develops the theme of "you-appeal".

CHAPTER FOUR

Tactics

When your preparation is complete, the great thing is to be ready to adapt your methods to the local terrain. Flexible responses are part and parcel of good tactics.

During the negotiations we explored various avenues, and finally came up with a solution which seemed mutually beneficial.

I took the sucker for a fortune, and the beautiful thing is he still doesn't know what happened.

> Two descriptions of the same event, delivered by the parties from opposite sides of the negotiating table.

In military terms, tactical warfare brings into play three variables: strength, position and the element of surprise. If politicians make policy, and the general staff are responsible for strategy, the line officers in the field live in the sphere of tactics. (It is the common soldiers' job to shoot straight, and the sergeants' job to keep them at it.)

If you ask three businesspeople to tell you how policy, strategy and tactics interrelate, you will get six different answers. "Tactics", particularly, changes according to the context in which you find it—it is a chameleon word.

The traveling businesspeople at whom we have aimed this chapter are somewhere between second lieutenant and colonel. Their span of control is tactical: they are mandated to make decisions of limited scope in "real time"—reacting to changing circumstances without reference back to HQ.

We hope it will become clear that we do not equate "real time" with "short term". One of the underlying messages in this chapter is this: Every tactical decision made on the spot should contribute to longer-term, strategic objectives. If a field officer engages and defeats an enemy patrol, but sparks off a major battle that his own side is not prepared for, he can't expect any medals.

The other message of this chapter is: Understanding and respecting your business partner's needs does not mean weakness or sentimentality. It means good business.

Learning How to Negotiate

The first half of this book has been largely devoted to exploring the background to communication. When you have done your homework on your potential partner's background (culture,) acquainted yourself with the *company* or departmental context he comes from, and paid due consideration to his *character* (our three constant factors), you are ready to start considering your *tactics* (the first of our transient factors). Up to this point, it makes little difference whether you are preparing for a stand-up presentation, a working lunch, or a crucial round of golf.

We find that it is specifically the use of the word "negotiation" in the title of a book or seminar which raises expectations in the area of "tactics". The reader or participant wants to become more competent tactically, by learning frameworks and ground rules to give shape to his or her own general experience and common sense. People are given to saying "I'm something of an amateur psychologist" without ever having read a book on the subject; similarly, they like to think of themselves as quite smart tacticians who need a little professional coaching.

Books available on negotiation are legion, and they set the tone for the seminars. There is no doubt that the clients for both are motivated by self-interest in one form or another: nobody has yet produced a business bestseller entitled *How To Be More Generous* or *How To Give The Other Guy More and Take Less Yourself.* Conversely, we have yet to come across a course in "How to cheat, lie and retire early", or "How to trample the other guy under foot". The promotional leaflets tend to feature handshakes rather than clenched fists, and the "win:win" approach is usually favored: if we can find a way to enlarge the pie, we can both get a bigger piece.

This "green negotiator" ideal fits the spirit of the times, and the management training courses we run in many countries confirm that the vintage travels well. The participants, from anywhere in the world, quickly learn that "give and take" is different from "push and pull", and that nice guys need not be losers.

A "Pure" Negotiation

This is an exercise of classic simplicity, used by game theorists and negotiation analysts to explore questions of trust/suspicion, appeasement/aggression and forgiveness/punishment.

Two players, A and B, are each offered the choice of bidding X or Y. Both are aware of the scoring system:

A bids	B bids	A scores	B scores
X	X	3	3
X	Y	1	4
Y	X	4	1
Y	Y	2	2

Bids are simultaneous, and the score is added up after each round.

(If you want to run it yourself, have A and B sit back to back, each equipped with a pair of flash cards—X and Y, or Red and Blue. Each player holds one card aloft on the command "Bid!" from the referee. The scoreboard should be visible to both.)

In a typical game of 10 rounds, then, there are 60 points potentially available for distribution—both players bidding X throughout, and scoring 10 × 3 each. Of course, this produces neither "winner" nor "loser", but a high score for both players.

This "perfect score" rarely happens. Players are slow to see that X + X = *benefits for all* equation, and often even slower to implement it, since bidding X entails a risk—not only of forsaking one point, but also of permitting the "enemy" to develop a three-point lead.

A comparative analysis (Carlisle and Parker, *Beyond Negotiation*) focused on precisely this: how early in the game, if ever, will a player bid X? The comparison, made over several thousand runs of the game, was between British and American players.

Before you read the next paragraph, close your eyes and think: which of the two cultures is more likely to play in the spirit of "I win—you lose (...avoid X bids)?"

In the first round, 27 percent of American players bid X, as against only 15 percent British. Within the first four rounds, 80 percent of Americans took the risk at least once, as against only 40 percent of British.

So, did you guess right? What stereotype or model were you drawing on?

"Uncertainty tends to produce conservative behavior", observes Carlisle, and goes on to speculate about the British class system leading to ingrained mutual suspicion between employers and unions, and thence between customers and suppliers. If that hypothesis is not sufficient to explain this apparently destructive pattern of behavior among British players: "There is another conjecture: that the British do not really wish to take responsibility for a long-term relationship which is of relative equality. They actually prefer the arm's-length relationship, not because it is, on the face of it, more cost effective, but because they cannot risk 'getting involved'....It is safer to 'play games' ".

By this interpretation, the *playing the game* idea which is traditionally associated with the British is not necessarily a creative way of securing the best deal for everybody.

It is worth noting that the evidence for these conclusions was a set of results from within each culture—British negotiating with British, Americans with Americans. Our own observations have usually been of negotiations between cultures. The transactions we have observed usually involve more complicated factors than the game described here.

The exercise, known as "The Prisoners' Dilemma", is rich in source material for the behavioral scientist. Dissertations have been written, television programs produced, and computer models developed. Computer simulation reveals that the most successful strategy long-term is tit-for-tat: open with an X (offering to be a Nice Guy) and then mirror the other player's bids (avoiding becoming a Victim). It opens the way to healthy scoring and and protects you from too heavy a beating by Y bids.

Meanwhile, in those rounds where you meet another Nice Guy, you can profit from each other's cooperative approaches.

So in the long term, the Nice Guys as a group tend to rise to the top, leaving the others behind in a welter of mistrust.

Know Your Own Attitude

You must become a new kind of Scandinavian. You must develop the killer instinct. You must learn to love manipulating people.

> Human Resource Director in a major
> Swedish company, addressing the
> latest intake of university graduates

Comments like these provide clues to a person's view of business: "He's a great engineer, but he's too honest to make a good salesman"; "I'm worried about your attitude—you seem to be determined to tell the client the truth, even when she hasn't asked for it"; "It's one big game, so don't get all tangled up in ethics"; "Tell them what they want to hear, that's the trick"; "It's dog eat dog out there".

Where do you draw the line between persuasion and manipulation? Between manipulation and cheating? Unless you have a fairly clear view of your own values, limitations and sticking points, you are a danger to yourself in negotiations.

Of course, if you *are* out for a quick killing, you must have that clear in your mind from the outset. Uncertainty guarantees failure.

Yet being nice, building a reputation for honesty, is not simple dumb altruism. Typically, a mature business gets 80 percent of its orders from established clients, and this puts a premium on good long-term relationships.

Choose Your Weapons

Nevertheless, people do have an appetite for the quick and easy route. *How To Succeed in Business Without Really Trying* was a great hit in the 1960s.*

When we run negotiations seminars, we often include a session on "Dirty Tricks". Participants seem to look forward to this with special enthusiasm. To be fair, it isn't always that they want to add to their own armory. Rather, they want to learn how to respond effectively if a business partner starts playing dishonest games.

So here is a short list of upsetting maneuvers you might encounter in some form. In each case, we have suggested a response that might bring the negotiation back onto a more fair and open footing.

1. "Your Competitor..."

He says: "Of course I've had a much better offer elsewhere...". He hopes to beat you down.

---

*A tongue-in-cheek management manual, later a musical and a film, by Shepherd Mead, 1952.

Response: You say, "So tell me about this other offer", or "I know there is good competition, but I'm convinced we are better". But both these tend to draw the conversation towards the competition. So a better reply is "If you've had a better offer elsewhere, and you're still talking to us, there must be something in our offer you like. Tell me about it."

2. "If It Was Up To Me..."

She says: "My boss would never agree to this...". She hopes to avoid making a decision.

Response: Salespeople are trained to talk to decision makers whenever possible, so "Let me talk to your boss, then" seems obvious. In many cultures, it can be counterproductive, causing loss of face (in Japan, for example), or resentment (in Germany). A more effective comeback is "That suggests you personally like the offer. Why don't we identify together the most appealing aspects, and then perhaps I can help you to present the case to your boss, making the most of these strong points."

3. "Sub-Clause 14B..."

He takes a hard line on an aspect of the deal that he doesn't really care about. He hopes to distract you from more important issues, and disguise his own priorities. (A sign of a quite advanced negotiator.)

Response: Probe with open questions: "Why is this so important to you?"; "Where does the issue fit into your scheme of things?"

4. "My Colleague Could Turn Nasty..."

The bad guy leans on you. The good guy offers tea and sympathy. "Why don't you concede, to save all this unpleasantness?" They hope to disorientate you, confuse you, and break down your defenses.

Response: Not easy. First, recognize the technique for what it is. Labeling it in your own mind can ease the psychological pressure

("Hmmm. The old bad guy/good guy game. I wonder if they swap roles occasionally…"). In the same spirit, you might go on to bring the thing right into the open: "I feel there's some bad atmosphere here"; "I'm getting mixed messages from you two".

5. "Oh, Were You Serious…?"

Just as a successful conclusion is in sight, she says: "Oh, but that was just a hypothetical understanding; we didn't actually agree to it." She hopes to gain time or avoid commitment in the hope of an improvement in the market…

Response: "Well, let's agree to it now, shall we?" (A well set up agenda should prevent this happening. More about agendas in Chapter 5.)

6. "And Gift-Wrapped, of Course…"

It's all settled. Then, with pen poised for signing, he asks for that extra little something. Or is it so little? He hopes to take advantage of your eagerness to clinch the deal.

Response: Ask for something in return—even if it's only an unspecified favor in the future: "OK, OK, but just this once. And I'm going to remember that you owe me one…".

7. "I Can't Waste Any More Time…"

She threatens to walk out. Is she bluffing? If so, she hopes to put pressure on you to improve your offer—to hold a pistol to your head, in other words.

Response: Call her bluff. Let her go, but keep channels open: "Goodbye, then. I feel we've been making real progress, so I'll get back to you."

Overall, then, a firm, straightforward response to such tricks will win you control in the short run and respect in the long.

American comic books have long carried advertisements for martial arts correspondence courses: "Learn Iron Fist defense techniques in five easy lessons, and you can overcome up to three attackers in a dark alley". It took Woody Allen to point out the absurdity: what if the bad guys have also taken the Iron Fist course?

So far in this chapter, we have been dealing with matters tactical at the universal level—truths that apply anywhere and everywhere. We now tighten the focus to see what happens when the tacticians are from different cultural backgrounds.

Know Your Partner's Attitude

Outside the training center and the seminar suite, we hear stories of shady dealing from the people we meet along the way ("You train people in negotiations, do you? Here's one for you: a friend of mine…well, a friend of a friend, actually, but anyway…").

We have been involved in conversations, particularly in the airport bar at Helsinki, where the Nordic sauna has been discussed. There is a commonly held view that an invitation to the sauna has a more sinister purpose than simple hygiene and relaxation. "It's a way of breaking down your resistance, you see. They're used to seeing each other with nothing on, so they know they're at an advantage—a territorial thing. Anyway, how can you maintain your dignity in the next day's negotiations if you think they've been comparing notes about your anatomy?"

Similarly with the Russians and alcohol. "That banquet on the last day! Eight glasses lined up beside each plate, for different types of vodka. We'd been warned, of course. All designed to get you drunk and then catch you off your guard. It's water being poured into the other side's glasses."

The sauna is an important social focus in Finland. Formal hospitality in Russia demands lots of toasts. Those who claim to have detected ulterior motives are actually telling us quite a lot about their own hang-ups.

There are, of course, massive local variations in what is ethical or respectable in business; different cultures have different thresholds for trickery, confrontation and gamesmanship.

Uneven Playing Fields

Sure, I've got a lot of time for the "win:win" school. Only trouble is, when one of these kids comes up against an "I win:you lose" merchant—some caveman who can't even *spell* Harvard—then you get zero communication. They're playing different games.

Senior executive, Port of New York
Authority

Peter Sellers is immensely popular in Sweden, but one of his classic films was never released there: *I'm All Right, Jack*—in which he portrays Fred Kite, union shop steward in England's dark days of class war and demarcation dispute. We ran the film once for a group of Stockholm businesspeople, to gauge their reaction: which was perplexity and horror in equal amounts. Not funny at all. This was socially insane behavior: nonproductive conflict.

After the turmoil in France in 1968, the government promised many reforms, including a loosening of its grip over television, which many radicals saw as a propaganda tool for whichever party was in power. They looked across the Channel to study the apparently much healthier situation in the United Kingdom. To their consternation, they found that the British government had even greater powers over the BBC according to the BBC's charter than had the French government over ORTF. The point was that no British government had ever used those powers to the full. The observers concluded that such a system (or lack of system) could not work in France. The French use a franglais word—*le fairplay*—to describe the British arrangement.

(If this example of harmony and understanding in British institutions seems to contradict the Peter Sellers example which precedes it, consider the class system and its effects: the government in Whitehall and the BBC's upper echelons were predominantly staffed—some would say they still are—by members of a class élite. "Fair play" meant little in the world of Fred Kite—or if it did, it did not apply to his dealings with those from outside his own class.)

Outsiders can fare badly in negotiations with Far Eastern cultures which are rooted in Confucianism. The system has, at its heart, strict ideas of filial piety and duty both upwards and downwards. The vertical bonds that run father-to-son-to-grandson are exclusive; no matter how you handle yourself during business dealings, you cannot become your trading partner's son or father. There is no code of conduct for "proper" dealings with outsiders, and so xenophobia has a free rein. In Japan there is a saying: *Hito-wo mitara doroboro omoe* (Treat a stranger like a thief.).

The *gwailoh* (long-nosed devil) negotiating with the Chinese sometimes experiences rough treatment. It is said that a recent Hong Kong governor suffered a heart attack in Beijing during negotiations over 1997. The Chinese delegation listened to his side's point of view in silence for a while, and then suddenly exploded in an unstoppable torrent of vituperation. This style of negotiation is not "win:win", it is "I win: you can take care of yourself if you like."

Japan was closed to foreigners for 265 years up to 1868. During that time, the Japanese learned strict control of their facial expressions and body language, enabling them in the last 120 years to suppress any distaste they feel at dealing with *gaijin* (foreigners). This is just as well, for where China is self-sufficient in all raw materials, Japan has a transformation economy, so its representatives must always be prepared to seek out the best deal with foreign suppliers or customers. If this attitude leads to a "win:win" contract, then well and good—but it will be for reasons of pragmatism, rather than from any desire to "do the right thing" by the stranger.

The refined principle of group decision making so typical of Japan's overcrowded island carries the label *wa* (harmony). It expresses itself most obviously in quiet speech, modest conduct, and refined good manners. We have worked with many Japanese preparing for long postings to Europe or the United States, and know well the difficulty they have in saying "no" to a business partner's face. This inhibition is not present in the Chinese.

Know Your Partner's Bargaining Range

The street markets of the world are thronged with nervous tourists: What are the rules hereabouts? Am I supposed to wave my arms around and shout? What's the mark-up on an Aztec flute?

Back home, if you have an antique to sell, you can go to auction (in which case the auctioneer lets the market of bidders decide the value

of the article), sell it yourself (if you can find a purchaser), or negotiate with a dealer (who will be out to secure the fattest possible margin).

> *Novice:* "I've changed my mind. It's too big for the downstairs bath-
> room. Can I have my money back?"
> *Dealer:* "I can give you six hundred dollars for it."
> *Novice:* "But I paid you a thousand only an hour ago!"
> *Dealer:* "Buying and selling are two different things. I thought everybody
> knew that."

No "Dirty Trick" here. The dealer has to pay the rent on his shop,
and only sells two pieces a week. If our novice had given this a moment's thought, he would have taken that Art Nouveau screen on
approval for a few days, rather than actually buying it outright. The
dealer would have agreed readily—he knows the value of a relationship.

Businesspeople, particularly in the service sector, often prefer
dealing with experienced partners, who understand how the mar-
gins work, and so can bargain in an informed and efficient way.

The restaurateur winces when she overhears: "Look at these wine
prices! I saw this one in the supermarket yesterday for half that!
That's a lot of money for pulling a cork out!"

The freelance management consultant takes a deep breath before
he names his daily rate. So many clients choose to forget everything
they ever knew about costings, and assume that the consultant is
pocketing the whole sum, free of overheads, tax and pension contri-
bution—and that he is making that kind of money 365 days a year.

Manage Your Own Bargaining Range

If he asks for ten, he means eight and he wants six. So it's worth
four. Offer two.

> Traditional advice to those about to
> visit the casbah

The seller of carpets does not want you to know too much about
what he's up to. There he sits, just where he always sits, surrounded by

his merchandise and sipping tea. How can you know what he wants out of the deal? Is he hungry for turnover at the moment? Or is profit the issue? It is unlikely that he will lower his price so as to add your name to his client list....

But not every business partner is as inscrutable as the carpet seller. If you use a little imagination and do a little asking around, you can tunnel into the other's motivation, and shape your offer accordingly.

A classic case, particularly when dealing with large (dare we say "bureaucratic"?) companies, is the partner who wants to look good in her boss's eyes. Let us make her the purchaser, and you the salesperson.

Now your goods: a piece of personal computer hardware that she might want to buy in bulk, and sell to the public through her firm's shopping center outlets. You can offer not only the machines, but training for sales staff, training for after-sales service staff, point-of-sale publicity material, advertising support both nationally and locally, a stock of spare parts, etc.

Now the question: when you first name your price, do you:

1. name the basic, no-frills price of the machine, and add the other items piecemeal? or

2. name a price for the whole package as the first step?

Option 1 has major drawbacks. To allow yourself negotiating latitude you have to name a high price for the basic minimum purchase, and that might alienate the buyer from the start. And you must allow yourself negotiating latitude, or else she won't be able to compress your price and report victory to her boss.

If you go for 2, you can have a creative series of meetings, trimming a little here and a little there off the ancillary items: "OK, let's see what happens if we just print the promotional material in two colors...". You watch the overall price creep down and down at no real cost to anybody, but to your purchaser's enormous satisfaction.

This approach is equally common in the turnkey project arena, where it is known as "technical compression".

We are not suggesting that this particular tactic applies in your industry or profession. We have omitted many variables: the state of the market; the competition's practices; the personal relationship between seller and buyer. Yet the point is illustrated: before you go into the meet-

ing, check your offer to make sure there are sufficient areas of flexibility.
Then you can trim and mold it as the negotiations proceed.

Shape Your Tactics to Suit Your Partner

The best, most subtle tactics are based on an understanding of the
other party's motivations, taking into account factors of background
culture, business context, and individual character.

The Man Who Never Was, the true story of a counter-intelligence
plot, includes the following paragraphs concerning a plan to confuse the enemy with a misleading document:

> You are a British Intelligence Officer; you have an opposite number in
> the enemy Intelligence, say (as in the last war), in Berlin; and above him
> is the German Operational command. What you, a Briton with a British
> background, think can be deduced from a document does not matter.
> It is what *your opposite number,* with his German knowledge and back-
> ground, will think that matters—what construction he will put on the
> document. Therefore, if you want him to think such-and-such a thing,
> you must give him something which will make him (and not you)
> think it.
>
> But he may be suspicious and want confirmation; you must think
> out what enquiries will he make (not what enquiries would you make)
> and give him the answers to those enquiries so as to satisfy him. In other
> words, you must remember that a German does not think and react as
> an Englishman does, and you must put yourself into his mind.

Case Study

The Danish salesman knew his machine well, and he knew it could
turn out 10,000 egg cartons an hour working at full capacity.

The Soviet factory manager liked the machine, knew its capacity,
and had insisted on an extension of the guarantee period: any running
faults in the first three years, and a Danish engineer would be flown
out to fix it—at the expense of the supplier.

"So, all is agreed, then. My congratulations. Now, if you can stand
it, I would like to invite you to one further meeting tomorrow. Concerning the maximum productive capacity."

"Of course, but I thought everything was clear."

"Between you and me, yes. But there will be another person at the meeting tomorrow—a representative from the regional collective. When I ask you how many units per hour the machine will turn out, I suggest you adjust your answer."

"Above 10,000, I'm afraid, things will start to go wrong."

"You see, this representative will set my production targets next year. And higher targets the year after. If we *start* at 10,000, we can be sure of breakdowns very soon—meaning production hold-ups for me, and great expense for you under the terms of the guarantee."

"I see. How would 8,000 sound?"

"Exactly the figure I had in mind."

The Soviet was buying more than an egg carton machine. He was buying a couple of years free of stress in the centrally planned economy.

Live for the Day After Tomorrow

Tactics are mainly to do with action in the short term. But the skillful tactician keeps a clear eye on the long-term effects.

Good tactics may even include the sacrifice of some small immediate gain in the name of a long-term relationship.

Case Study

It's 2 AM. An American salesman and his Spanish client stroll through the cobbled alleyways of ancient Toledo, their conversation ranging from the marvels of the city's architecture, to the impact of the European Union on the Spanish economy, to the personal foibles of business acquaintances—including the Spaniard's CEO, who is to put in an appearance at tomorrow's meeting.

Not a natural nightbird, the American is apprehensive. Is he being softened up before the crucial stages of the negotiation? It was certainly a good dinner…

Next day, the CEO cuts the proposal to ribbons beneath the pitying gaze of the salesman's host, who escorts the victim to the airport. "Don't worry. All that's needed is a price-cut, so Mr. Big can feel his intervention was effective…"

Sure enough, after a cosmetic adjustment in the terms, the deal is agreed by fax and phone within a week—delivery immediate, payment on the nail.

The faint odor of plastic warmed by halogen lighting. The office of a West German middle manager, who throws a barrage of objections at the American offer: "How can this possibly work?...incompatible with procedures...this is too extensive...that is insufficient...this we already have...that we do not need..."

The wipe-clean day planner on the wall allocates 45 minutes, and the salesman is duly shown out, clutching an armful of technical brochures as consolation. Correspondence continues for 18 months before any German commitment is made.

The salesman's worries during that time include: Why did they seem to understand so little about our service? What do they really think of our price? Why are they taking so long to decide?

Both Spanish and German deals resulted from successful negotiations. Similar product, same salesman. Two rather different countries, just one day's drive apart.

The variations between the two experiences fall into four categories:

- relationship

- hierarchy

- timing

- price/specification.

The *relationship* in the Spanish case was based on a strong degree of personal intimacy before any real business started. The local style is first to develop trust—chatting, sharing little secrets, spending hours over meals together—before the pocket calculators come out. Even then, every opportunity is taken to make the personal bond even tighter between the two people, as opposed to the two organizations.

In the German case, there was a cup of coffee as commercial discussions began. Much later, when business (and repeat business) was being done, the American was invited for chummy evenings in German homes—a form of business hospitality much more common there than in Spain.

A *hierarchy* was manifest in the Spanish set-up: the big boss came to show his authority (and size the salesman up). The CEO never appeared again after the first chilly meeting. He had served his purpose as the mouthpiece of the company. In the German case, authority had been delegated in a neat package: Investigate this supplier; if OK, report back; if not OK, look for others. The real decision maker was beyond the salesman's reach, and only broke cover at a later stage in the dealings.

Timing worked very differently in the two countries. In Toledo, there was a full day of discussion (on top of the previous evening's entertainment), during which the agenda suggested by the American salesman was warmly received, then largely ignored. Quick results thereafter. In Cologne, the 45-minute meeting adhered to the agreed timetable point by point, but left a great deal of exploration still to be done before a deal could be struck. (Much more about timing in Chapter 5.)

The German negotiator paid great attention to the *specification*, seeking weak points, and making it clear that his company would impose their requirements in certain areas before any deal was remotely possible. Fairly late in the proceedings, he asked for a *price*, remarked that it was in the higher range of his expectations, and made no attempt to bring it down.

His Spanish counterparts seemed to assume that their would-be suppliers knew their job, and were content to leave the detailed specifications to them. The pressure was all on price. The American company came close to losing the deal because they had made a firm price statement rather early and left themselves short of maneuvering space.

Culture Check

From tactics to tact is but a short step, and that brings us to good manners.

We chose 15 rules which can apply to everyday business behavior and asked panels of executives from a number of countries to rank them in order of importance—in response to the following stimulus:"If a visitor comes to your country to do business, and wants to fit in with the local style, what rules of conduct apply?"

The rules are set out below in random order. There are many games you can play with the list, but we suggest that you use the first column to rank the items for your own native culture, then subsequent columns for your guesses at one or more target cultures.

The commentary below contains the experts' (i.e., natives') answer from France, Germany, Italy, Switzerland, Sweden, Japan, Spain, Hungary and Britain, using several dozen respondents in each case, averaged out.

When you turn to the commentary to check your grade, the thing to look for is big deviations (five or greater) between your ranking and the locals' ranking for any given item. Then give it some thought or, better, pick the brains of the next native of that country you meet: you might have been getting something wrong…

Remember: 1: Most important; 15: Least important.

Your country		*Target countries*	
_____	Talk about business only	_____	_____
_____	Understand local economic trends	_____	_____
_____	Make quick decisions	_____	_____
_____	Show interest in host's family	_____	_____
_____	Be patient	_____	_____
_____	Arrive exactly on time for meetings	_____	_____
_____	Smile	_____	_____
_____	Choose local food	_____	_____
_____	Have good local introductions	_____	_____
_____	Accept invitations to go drinking	_____	_____
_____	Be prepared to work late	_____	_____

_____ Understand local politics   _____ _____
_____ Learn the language   _____ _____
_____ Dress carefully for meetings   _____ _____
_____ Say what you think directly   _____ _____

Commentary

(From left to right: France, Germany, Italy, Switzerland, Sweden, Japan, Spain, Hungary, Britain.)

	F	D	I	CH	S	J	E	H	GB
Business only	12	14	12	12	6	14	14	14	13
Economic trends	1	2	1	2	2	2	1	1	6
Decide quickly	2	5	3	3	3	8	7	6	9
Host's family	14	12	13	13	14	13	12	10	14
Patience	7	10	5	7	4	3	6	4	5
Be on time	3	1	9	1	1	1	8	5	3
Smile	6	13	10	9	11	5	10	9	4
Local food	15	15	15	15	13	15	15	13	15
Introduction	4	3	2	5	8	10	2	2	7
Go drinking	13	11	14	14	12	4	13	8	11
Work late	10	9	7	9	10	6	3	15	8
Politics	8	7	6	10	9	11	5	3	10
Language	5	6	4	11	15	7	4	12	1
Dress	11	4	11	4	7	12	9	11	2
Directness	9	8	8	6	5	9	11	7	12

Like all statistics on attitudes and behavior, the data in this table should be treated with caution. We have highlighted noteworthy highs and lows.

Remember that these rankings represent each nationality's view of itself—and to some extent the way each nationality would like itself to be viewed by outsiders. Some of the results surprised us, not fitting our own models of the countries concerned: e.g., D—Directedness; I—Dress; J—Introductions.

Nevertheless, the patterns that emerge are generally confirmed by outsiders—such as expatriates with long working experience in the cultures listed.

CHAPTER FIVE

Timing

In global dealings, time is the most noticeable aspect of distance. As you travel, take into account the shifting attitudes to time. When you arrive, make your arrangements about time to fit the local mood.

The clock, not the steam engine, is the key machine of the modern industrial age.

L. Mumford

Potatoes, enclosed in a black box, still respond chemically to the changes of night and day outside. Oysters, removed from their natural waters to a distant laboratory, maintain their feeding rhythms to match favorable tidal times "back home". Jet lag is a problem for some international executives. All living things have an internal clock.

Man has taken practical measurements of passing time from nature: the solar year, the lunar month (or some calendar compromise), night and day. The hour, the minute and the second were conceived of in Ancient Babylon, but they couldn't measure them. Roman hours varied in length with the season: there were always 12 hours to the night.

Until the eighteenth century, the time of day was largely a local concern. The village clock was set in accordance with its longitudinal position—which dictated the rising and the setting of the sun as the Earth spun on its axis—and if all agreed that the village clock was correct, that was good enough. The mail-coach system, moving fast enough to cause a problem with time, solved the problem by issuing the coachman with a clock that could be set to gain or lose as he traveled between villages. De Quincey wrote of "the conscious presence of a central intellect that in the midst of vast distance, of storms, of darkness, of danger—overruled all obstacles into one steady cooperation to a national result."

The clockmakers were also encouraged for supranational reasons. The Spanish and the English monarchs offered prizes for ever more accurate chronometers—not to work out what time it was at a fixed point on the globe, but rather the reverse: being sure what time it was, navigators could be more sure of where they were. A crossing to Jamaica in 1762 shipped a chronometer accurate to within five seconds.

A century later, "local time" and "railroad time" operated side by side in the United States—often with more than one railroad time in operation at busy interchanges like Pittsburgh. Time zone formalities were adopted in the United States in 1883. A year later, the world accepted Greenwich Mean Time as a global reference point—

partly in recognition of British flair in chronometry. That flair was closely linked with the Royal Navy's mastery of the sea.

Not all the world accepted GMT unhesitatingly, however. Germany only abolished its five internal time zones in 1891, and France resisted cross-Channel time until 1911. Since then the story has been one of increasing standardization and simplification. For philosophers and mathematicians, or in the rarefied atmosphere of physics, time might remain a complex puzzle to be solved, but for everyday practical purposes man has got time licked.

Yet time—and the way it is handled—is still a troublesome area of friction between individuals and cultures.

Time and Courtship

Social observers in the early 1940s found a strange mixture of attitudes among young people in the South West of England. Almost all the young men were American—servicemen based there during the build-up to the Normandy invasion. The young women were either local girls, or teenagers evacuated from the vulnerable cities.

Small-town America, at that period, was not notable for a climate of sexual freedom or loose living, yet the boys soon earned a reputation for being "fast". The English girls they were dating, meanwhile, were described back on the base as "easy", although the girls' families were certainly quite respectable, and there was a clear distinction between "a nice girl" and a tramp.

The observers investigated.

They found that there were approximately 30 stages of courtship, in both cultures, from first eye contact to full sexual intercourse. However, kissing came much earlier—was more "innocent"—in the American than in the English arrangement (say step 5 as opposed to 25).

So there was confusion over "how far do you go and how fast?" The American boy, claiming a kiss on the first date, did not feel he was pushing his luck. The English girl had to choose: slap his face, or offer more than either he or she had originally intended. Probably the slapped faces were not reported back at camp.

Differing attitudes to time lead to a great deal of unnecessary distress.

Set Your Watch to Local Time

I used to go to Yugoslavia quite a lot. It would take me about
three days each trip to slow down to the Balkan pace of life, and
I felt really bad tempered until I'd made the adjustment. Eventually, I trained myself consciously to adjust my body clock, tran-
quilizing myself as the JAT pilots scraped over the Alpine
summits with inches to spare.

Bill Reed, Director, Canning International Management Development

The case study in Chapter 4—that of the salesman in Germany and
Spain—touched on the central issue here: what comes first, business
or people? The answer is never straightforward, as the two consider-
ations are so closely intertwined.

The Westerner on a temporary assignment in Japan goes through
stages: "It's the same for everybody. Six days here and you're terribly
confused. Another six months and you're ready to write a book explaining it all. Six years after that you're terribly confused…"

Look beneath the superficial frenzy of life in the big Japanese
cities, and you find long working days (12 hours is typical) and long
careers (a lifetime in the same company). They use the time to build
harmonious agreements upon harmonious relationships.

Which means, effectively, putting people first. Somewhere between the apparently inconclusive meetings and the final business decision, the Western visitor may feel he or she is wasting yet more time
on dinners and drinking sessions during the hours of *breiko* after the
official working day is over. But that time is far from wasted. The
rather stiff conventions of office life fall away, and the people can get
in touch with each other.

If the business proposal under consideration now means working
together in the future the Japanese feel that no decision can be taken
until the people involved know each other. This does not mean that
the entertainments in the geisha house or karaoke bar are a specific
test. It simply makes sense to have these bonding experiences as part
of the development of a good working relationship.

It takes time to build, but it's powerful once it's in place. I recently had the opportunity to do a deal in Japan without consulting my partner there. Not with his direct competitors or anything, just a piece of business in the same market. I had to offer it to him first, although it wasn't really his sort of deal. He would have been horrified if the first he'd known was seeing the goods in the store. We've taken years to build this trust, and you don't just throw it away.

Italian manufacturer of kitchen
equipment

The German approach to time is highly structured with careful scheduling. Delegation, although practiced with thoroughness, usually has strings attached. This can make innovative decisions painful, as the subordinate's decision time with the boss is kept separate from his or her communication time with you. The junior has full authority over an agreed range of decisions, but that range can never include the unexpected. If he or she takes the conservative path, and blocks the upward progress of your surprise proposal ("I am not empowered to bring this matter to my boss's attention"), you are stuck. Even if you try the back door, and the boss likes the idea, the boss will be reluctant to overrule the subordinate. The economic emergency of the post-war years, when rules were frequently broken in order to get an urgent job done, was a long time ago.

The German attitude to time is changing. They leave the office on time and award themselves generous holidays.

Japanese competition is really unfair. We work efficiently; they work efficiently *and long*.

Senior manager, German car firm

Speed in decision making is in inverse proportion to bureaucracy. North American industry is often hung on top-down decision-making systems; "why change a winning formula?" is a rhetorical question most frequently asked by the man at the top who invented the formula. For all their protestations about time being money, American middle managers frequently disappoint by their hesitations and procrastination.

About the only thing that really does move faster in U.S. industry is the revolving door marked In and Out. There's really no stigma attached when the company lets you go...some ways it has a kind of cachet about it: "I was a real risk-taker, see, and I took one risk too many."

American manager, currently running ice-cream plant in New Jersey

Steady Sweden, on the other hand, where you never see anybody running along a corporate corridor, scores well on power delega-tion. The social systems are based on consensus, and this is reflected in a general absence of fear in the ranks of the big companies.

I give the matter due thought, and then, within reasonable limits, agree to what seems right to me. There are very few sanctions against me if I make a mistake—who ever gets sacked in Sweden?

Training manager, light engineering
firm, Malmö

We have heard Swedes at international conventions criticize their American colleagues for moving too slowly. It must be said, however, that carrots are also in short supply in Sweden, just as sticks are. There is little inducement to move particularly fast.

Spain is dramatically changing gear. With the highest sustained growth rate in Europe for the past few years, business there is in a hurry. Apart from less industrialized areas like Andalusia and Galicia, the stereotypical *mañana* image is completely, probably irreversibly, out of date.

Yet the traditions of hospitality, and pleasure in unhurried con-versation, persist. The commonest error among business visitors to Spain is to interpret this as a symptom of a lackadaisical attitude over-all. Beware. Once the essentials (taking care of people, primarily) have been dealt with, decisions are swift and action energetic.

Energy and decisiveness characterized the British in Queen Vic-toria's day. Amiability and procrastination are their hallmarks nowa-days. Holland and Britain are near neighbors, both geographically and culturally:

We have no difficulty getting on with our British colleagues, they're much the same as us—except they do go on about weather and the motorways for ages before getting down to business.

> Dutch engineer in petroleum
> company

Timing in the Middle East often trips up the inexperienced negotiator from elsewhere. Social, business and general matters rub against each other in apparently random order—a kind of "circular agenda" is the best description. A point will arise, get an airing, and then vanish, only to resurface in a different form later in the discussion.

Your Arab partner operates in "real time" more readily than, say, a North European: he has no fixed objective, but a dazzling speed in producing and processing new options during the meeting.

Time Tricks

In Chapter 4 we listed seven "Dirty Tricks", with appropriate responses. Here is a similar list of possible points of tension. In these cases, the explanation is likely to lie in differing views of time, rather than in any hostile intent.

1. So Sorry to Keep You Waiting...

She leaves you in the hallway for what seems like a long, long time. Clearly she hopes to make you feel inferior, in preparation for bullying you.

Response: If you are visiting a time-stressed culture, you are probably wrong—she is simply busy, running behind schedule, and innocent of any crude psychological warfare. If you are visiting a culture with a more relaxed attitude, your suspicions are equally groundless, and you have failed to adjust your rhythms: in similar circumstances, he would be perfectly happy to wait. Either way, no response necessary.

2. I Don't Feel This Is the Right Moment...

He persistently refuses to address the key issue, giving no reason for his procrastination. Most likely he's playing for time...

Response: Convince yourself that he isn't up to anything. Quite possibly, he is just as lost in the cross-cultural time-warp as you are, and will be happy if you break the spell by saying: "I really think we must discuss it very soon", or "Could we agree on a time when we can discuss it?" Being firm is often the most polite course of action.

3. I Really Must Take You to See the Nougat Factory...

Her scheme seems clear. She wants to waste time until you are about to leave, and then pile the pressure on—knowing you would hate to go home empty-handed.

Response: Either "No, we really must get down to business now", or (if the deal is important enough) "Wonderful, my children love nougat—but before we go, could I just ring the airline to postpone my flight home?" Her "scheme" is probably in your imagination. Those who claim to have suffered from this trick usually set the scene in Eastern Europe—in the days when an overrun exit visa was a real disaster.

Quiz: Which Nationality Is the Object of These Comments?

1. "No good trying to telephone them on a Friday afternoon; they're all off to the islands for the weekend."

2. "A breakfast meeting, he suggested. Breakfast! Can you imagine!"

3. "She seemed to think sticking to the agenda was more important than solving the problem."

4. "Work hard? Yes, they work hard—if by that you mean spending long hours at the office…"

5. "The tea-break mentality. Drives you crazy!"

6. "The hardest thing I've ever been asked to do: they wanted me to make an after-dinner speech at 7pm."

7. "No, no. Any time but August. Forget August. Waste of time."

8. "In the cities, it's fine. But in the small towns in the valleys, it seems like every second day's a saint's day. No business."

9. "Bustle, bustle, bustle. Makes them feel important. But try to pin them down and what do you get? 'I can't decide without instructions from my boss, and he's away at a conference.'"

10. "Protestant work ethic? What does that mean nowadays? Get the job done so you can leave before the rush hour starts."

Answers

1. The Swedes

2. A Frenchman (who worked for an American company)

3. A Frenchwoman (who worked for a state-run bureaucracy)

4. The Japanese

5. The British

6. The Finns

7. The Italians

8. The Swiss

9. The Americans

10. The Germans

Culture Check

Here is a list of 20 words.

   If you have a companion to help you, ask him or her to read them out to you clearly, without any particular emphasis, at about one word per second. If you are alone, try to simulate the effect by running your eye slowly down the page, lingering for a second or so on each word.

Soft
   Catch
      Grape
         Four
            Losing
               Trend
                  Partly
                     Stamina
                        Gentle
                           Backwards
                              Skill
                                 Metric
                                    Score
                                       Breakfast
                                          Then
                                             Likely
                                                Rest
                                                   Aptitude
                                                      Chair
                                                         Push

Now turn to the section marked "Test" overleaf.

TEST

In this space, write down as many of the 20 words as you can remember.

No time limit—continue until you have dried up. Now check back to the original list to see which words you forgot.

As an individual, you are a small statistical sample, but you will probably find that you did better on the words near the beginning of the list, and towards the end. (This is if you are European or North American by background: otherwise, *see* "Local variation" on the next page.

The attention/retention curve for a typical audience (either of one or of a hundred) looks like this:

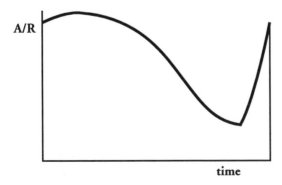

In practical terms this means that your listeners pay attention to what they are told at the beginning of a session, doze off a little after that (as every public speaker knows), and perk up again when the end is in sight.

As for retention, we meet here evidence of what psychologists call "primacy" and "recency". These factors affect memory over much longer time scales, too. When we cram for examinations at the end of a three-year course, we find the first term's work (primacy) and yesterday's input (recency) much fresher in our minds than the material we encountered a year ago.

The test you just ran on yourself lasted about 20 seconds. Twenty minutes is probably the longest useful time for a presentation.

Nobody wants the after-lunch slot on a day-long seminar. If you are stuck with it, change something: the lighting, the layout of the chairs, your visual aids. So one creates a series of peaks:

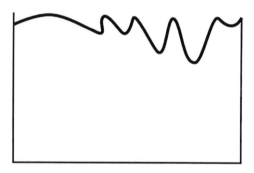

Local variation: Japan
Our Canning colleagues in Tokyo ran the 20-word exercise many times on Japanese business executives. The resulting curve averaged out like this:

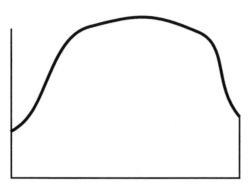

The overall pattern is virtually the reverse of what we have been seeing from Westerners.

An English management consultant who had sat through many Japanese presentations offered these explanations:

> The first thing to mention is the stress laid on rote learning in Japanese education. They do have very good aural retention. So that might give us a flat curve: they don't draw blanks the way we do.
>
> Now the peak in the middle—or rather the relatively poor performance at the two ends: what you get at these stages of a Japanese presentation is a lot of formalities with no real message. They like to spend the first part giving credit to everyone who has contributed—"*nemawashi** has happened"—and establishing their own right to be up there speaking. Everybody nods politely, but they're saving their "active listening" for the vital middle period—the meaty bit. Once that's over, it's back to the formalities...

Japanese friends were amazed at the Western curve: surely intelligent people can concentrate better than that?

---

*Nemawashi: the process of consultation so essential to Japanese decision making.

> The idea of "State your message, develop it, re-state it in your summary" was quite alien to them.
>
> Now I understand why my British colleagues become agitated when listening to Japanese speakers...
>
> Head of sales, Tokyo office of
U.K. pharma company

Agenda

Agenda Item One: The Agenda

Now think about this. When you were doing that attention/retention exercise, did it make any difference that you knew the length of the list (20 words, as we told you) in advance? Of course it did. If the list had been apparently endless, you would have been less able to manage your own mental processes.

In international dealings, well-designed agendas are useful even when they are unnatural in the local context. Circular agendas, and oblique approaches to problems, are fine if the communication between parties is subtle and highly developed. Often, however, there is some communication difficulty—language being the obvious example. In these cases overt, straight-line agendas are best. They reduce anxiety and promote understanding and free the mind to concentrate on what is important.

The Agenda Is on the Table. Is the Agenda on the Table?

The expression "hidden agenda" has become fashionable lately. We have heard it used as a synonym for "ulterior motive", as in "He asked me back to his place for coffee, but I think he had a hidden agenda."

We use the term as follows: your *hidden agenda* is the list of items in order of *importance* for you and your side. It might include some

Culture Check

You are setting up a meeting with a partner you know quite well, to discuss a bundle of issues. You are free to decide the running order of the following.

A. A point of technical detail with no immediate repercussions.
B. Some long-term thoughts you've been wanting to air.
C. A delicate item, difficult to agree on.
D. Immediate action points.
E. Good news for your partner.
F. A matter to be agreed, probably quickly and easily.
G. Bad news for your partner.

Think about it for a moment. Then write down the seven letters, in the running order you would favor:

Now take a look at our version below.

E. Good news first promotes a positive atmosphere. Anyway, to withhold it seems artificial.
G. Bad news next to get it out of the way. Again, keeping it until later in the meeting seems manipulative.
F. Easy negotiations now, to reestablish the lost momentum.
B. Long-term ideas, unlikely to spark conflict, establish a sense of trust to put the next item in context.
C. Delicate item.
A. Minor technical matter can be postponed if time runs short.
D. Immediate action points, likely to be affected by the foregoing, so keep them until last—where they are also likely to be remembered.

items which do not appear on the *open agenda,* which is the list of discussion points for the meeting, in order of *time.*

How to Handle Two Agendas

The banker's priorities differ from the client's, the salesperson's from the purchaser's, the HQ manager's from the country manager's, the boss's from the employee's. Contrasting cultures will make such differences even greater. Hidden agendas diverge.

Wonderful. If they ran parallel and close, never touching, there would be few opportunities for creative trade and exchange. So:

Clarify your own hidden agenda

Dig deeper into your own needs and desires. Perhaps you have been carried along by circumstances so fast that you have lost touch with your own, or your organization's, purpose. Be sure you know what really matters and what doesn't. This is especially important if you are negotiating as part of a team.

And theirs

Write down in note form everything you've gathered or guessed about their priorities. Shuffle your notes around to get a proper feeling for their needs.

Agree an open agenda first

This can often be done before the meeting (one of the best uses of the fax machine), with some fine tuning once the meeting begins—"Are we sure this agenda suits us both?" The purpose is not to impose discipline or save time, but to build confidence, demonstrate common interests, and open the road to agreement on matters of substance.

Allow time for exploration

Two ways of looking at the situation:

- My company has spent a lot of money flying me out here, so I must make sure no time is wasted, which means getting down to practicalities as quickly as we can. No time to waffle.

- My company has spent a lot of money flying me out here, so I must make sure we do the job properly, which means sounding out the other side thoroughly before we get down to practicalities. Otherwise we shall inevitably miss opportunities, and I might as well have stayed at home.

Then start trading

You can give something away that is insignificant on *your* hidden agenda, but more important to *them*. In return, they yield to you on a minor matter to them which is vital to you. You both finish with a gain at the cost of something trivial.

CHAPTER SIX

Talk

Talk is the point of contact. Speak clearly and listen closely, and agreement becomes possible. To be clear and convincing in the international arena requires special communication skills.

> *One can lie with the mouth, but with the accompanying grimace one nevertheless tells the truth.*
>
> Nietzsche

Talking and listening, at the sharp end of our pyramid, happen in real time. All your careful preparation can be wasted if the message is distorted at the moment of contact. So it is a good idea to do a little work on your message in advance. What sort of work do we mean?

In this chapter we will lead you to an understanding of how to shape your message to cross barriers of culture and language.

A World Language?

When Alexander the Great died in 323BC, his empire collapsed into bickering factions. They all bickered in Greek. A common form of Greek remained as the language of the Eastern Mediterranean for more than a thousand years.

The Roman legions marched across Western Europe, built their great straight roads, and spread the Latin language. When the Vandals ripped the heart out of the Empire (455AD), the roads and the language remained. As the roads crumbled away, the solders' dialect of Latin evolved into the Romance languages—French, Spanish, Portuguese, Romanian. Latin itself lived on as the language of the Roman church and the educated elite ("the ghost of the Roman Empire, sitting crowned upon the grave thereof", Gibbon). Until the Reformation, church Latin was standard from Bohemia to Ireland, and from Stockholm to Cadiz. Another empire was built by the conquistadors in Central and South America. Linguistically, it lives on; today over 200 million people outside Spain speak Spanish as their first language—a direct descendent of Latin in lands the Legions never knew.

The Arabic language travelled with Islam around the southern Mediterranean. Today, Arabic speakers outside the Arabian peninsula outnumber Saudi Arabians by 15 to 1.

In the eighteenth and nineteenth centuries, the intellectual and political prestige of France made French a contender for the title of "World Language". Educated people throughout the world learned

French as their first foreign language: the Russian aristocracy spoke it in preference to Russian.

German, too, came close to being a lingua franca. As German merchants and settlers established a network throughout Central Europe, from the early middle ages to the industrial revolution, theirs was the language of trade. (There is a widespread myth that German was nearly adopted as the language of the infant United States—that the proposal was defeated by just one vote in Congress. But it is only a myth.)

Being a lingua franca means much more than just the fact that "a lot of people speak it". Standard Chinese has the greatest number of native speakers in the world, and yet is understood and used by virtually nobody outside the native-speaking community.

So far, no other language has spread as far as English. Three factors have set English up as the world language: the Empire, the Merchant Navy, and the computer.

- The Empire left a string of English-speaking settlements in relatively empty lands such as Australia, New Zealand, Canada and the United States. In more populous territories, such as India and Africa, the English language has outlasted the Empire as the most convenient way to talk between communities. (There are at least 500 distinct languages in sub-Saharan Africa, and even more in the Indian subcontinent.) Today, English is an official language in 45 different countries, from Anguilla to Zimbabwe.

- During the British dominance of world trade in the nineteenth century, the Merchant Navy established the island's language, often in crude form, as the most reliable way to have a cargo loaded or unloaded in almost any port in the world. As British trade declined, the Americans moved in, speaking the same language—more or less.

- Thanks to the U.S. dominance of the computer industry in its early days, English provides the vocabulary for describing the machines and the jobs they do. As the great dictionaries of the world's languages appear in new editions and supplements, many of the new usages they list are in the area of computer science, and most of those usages spring from English.

A Language for Business

Shell, the Anglo-Dutch company, chose English as its language in the 1920s. After all, how many of the British managers spoke Dutch?

By the 1970s, it seemed natural that Chancellor Schmidt and Président Giscard d'Estaing, building European unity, should talk to each other in fluent English, even if the British were absent from the table.

When, in the late 1980s, Swedish ASEA and Swiss Brown Boveri became ABB, English was again the language of convenience—a language both Swedish and Swiss engineers could handle.

As the old regimes of Eastern Europe tumbled in 1989–90, and the new popular movements showed themselves to the world on television, there was always an English speaker on hand to address the microphones.

Similar instances abound. To speak in English is to speak to the world. The language has cut loose its moorings to the island of its origin.

As a French businessman put it: "The English language does not belong to the British and the Americans, you know."

English in the World Today

- 300 million speak English as their mother tongue;

- 800 million more put it to use daily;

- 75 percent of the world's mail is in English; as are

- 80 percent of the data stored on the world's computers, and

- 45 percent of the world's scientific publications.

The use of English is growing geometrically, and will probably only be limited by the number of people in the world. The need for a world language has never been so great.

Artificial Languages

Of course, there have also been attempts to *create* a world language. Esperanto, the best-known artificial language, was invented in the 1880s.

Twenty years ago, the Esperanto Society claimed eight million speakers in a hundred countries. Its advocates claim that the administrative life of the UN/the EC/the Olympic Committee would be transformed by the adoption of Esperanto. Their arguments, usually presented in English, fall on deaf ears.

In the 1930s a group of linguists and intellectuals promoted "Basic English", which trims the excess richness of English vocabulary, and irons out the more complex folds of its grammar.

(In fact derivatives of Basic English are quite widely used in technical documentation, to avoid confusion arising from the sloppy use of synonyms: "switch", "button", "knob", "control", "lever," "contact", "relay" and so on.)

Two forces work against artificially created languages. First, language is by its nature a slippery and undisciplined creature. The Académie in France is the object of wry amusement as it tries to keep the French language pure, and to stop the French people saying just what they feel like saying. Marcel insists on his right to go "footing" and drop off his "smoking" at the "pressing" ("jogging", "dinner jacket", and "dry cleaner's"). Any language designed by academics has only a slim chance of survival.

The second factor is a matter of headcount and investment. It is a long job, learning a language. From a zero start, the average adult must spend several hundred hours in dedicated study before he or she can hold even a straightforward conversation on an undemanding topic with a sympathetic partner. Hobbyists apart, such an effort is only worth while if there are lots of other people around with whom to speak the language.

Overseas English—Language of Convenience

In the rest of this book we will describe how overseas English is used as an effective tool in international business. It is aimed in two directions at once.

- First, if you are a native speaker of English, we give guidance on how to modify your way of speaking. As a master of the language,

DEFINITIONS

First language, native language, mother tongue: one learnt in childhood, and so the one in which the speaker normally thinks—hence "native speaker".

Dialect: a regional variant of a standard language in which grammar, vocabulary and accent are markedly different, but still comprehensible to the main community.

Patois: a dialect spoken in a small isolated region—e.g., mountain villages.

Pidgin: (corruption of the word "business") a way of speaking which mixes two or more languages together—typically by laying vocabulary from one over the grammar of another. Common in the Pacific, where English and Chinese mix. (*"Baiim Namba Wan Wailis!"* ("Buy the best radio!")—Sony slogan.)

Creole: a pidgin which has become a mother tongue. The vernacular of New Orleans is an example. (Probably from Portuguese *crioulo*—home-born slave).

Artificial language: one created by linguistic specialists.

Natural language: one created by its users over time.

Lingua franca: "mixture of Italian with French, Greek, Arabic, and Spanish, used in the Levant; any language serving as medium between different nations whose own languages are not the same; system providing mutual understanding. [It = Frankish tongue]" (*Concise Oxford Dictionary*)

Standard English: the English language as spoken by native speakers, such as varieties from the United States, Australia, etc.

Overseas English: our own term for the English language as spoken by people with other first languages, who have learnt it as adults, for practical rather than academic purposes.

you have the primary responsibility for the communication channel. It is you who must ensure that it is clean and free of extraneous noise.

- Secondly, if you are a non-native speaker, we suggest how you can make the maximum impact in English, and where you should concentrate your efforts as you work for improvement.

For both, we point out some of the common causes of misunderstanding.

In the *Cambridge Encyclopedia of Language*, David Crystal lays down six criteria for evaluating an international language. He had in mind artificial languages, but the questions raised are a valid test for this "evolved" language.

1. Easy to Learn

For the 310 million native speakers of Standard English, overseas English should be easy enough—requiring less investment of time and effort than a completely foreign language. That said, they have a poor record generally in communicating outside their own language group. There are skills involved in high-level overseas English which standard speakers sadly ignore. More of that later in this chapter.

For outsiders, English grammar is comparatively easy in the early stages—and overseas English goes little further than the early stages. There are no case or gender problems with nouns or adjectives ("The young man meets the young woman", and vice versa), and few verb changes ("I walked, you walked, they walked"). On the other hand, English spelling is a disaster area.

2. Relatable to Mother Tongues

Since English is a hybrid of Germanic and Latinate strains, there is some ease of access for Continental neighbors, Latin Americans, and francophone Africans. There are many points of contact in vocabulary, e.g.:

German	Fleisch	→	Flesh
Italian	Societa	→	Society

| Swedish | Fisk | → Fish |
| French | Chambre | → Chamber |

Further afield, but within the Indo-European language family:

Greek	Kyklos	→ Cycle
Russian	Voda	→ Water
Persian	Dokhtar	→ Daughter
Hindi	Raj	→ Royalty

For Hungarians, Finns, Japanese and others the going is tougher.

3. A Rich Range of Functions

Overseas English has evolved through use and has no set limits. Pop songs and papal blessings, table tennis tournaments and train timetables—all can be handled in overseas English. If not, overseas expands until they can, drawing on the wealth of standard English.

4. Standardized

Not yet. There is no authority to press it into a single mold. Yet the forces that have brought overseas English into being are still at work on it, and will tend to bring about harmonization and homogeneity. We predict a world in which a fairly universal overseas English is spoken, wherever administrators, technicians and tourists gather. But at home with their families they will continue to use their native tongues.

The Dutch and many Scandinavians already live this way. Fluent in English for all practical tasks, they keep their real mother tongue for more intimate or local concerns.

5. Neutral

Overseas English scores rather badly here. There are many who resent the world dominance of English, either because of a colonial past, or because they would like the world to be speaking French, German or whatever. Native English speakers should tread carefully, and never abuse their apparent advantage.

Former British Prime Minister, Margaret Thatcher visited Madrid in May 1989, and her schedule included a meeting with a senior minister who spoke excellent English. They had met before. High-level gossip in Spain was that he insisted on working through an interpreter the second time. The reason? At their previous meeting, the story went, Mrs. Thatcher had used cricket talk ("sticky wicket" and "bowl him a googly", presumably) in order to assert her dominance in the conversation.

We hope the story is not true; the important thing is that it was being told. As Spain has emerged into the European and global market, many Spaniards have had to work very hard to catch up in overseas English. (French being the traditional foreign language at school in Spain) and, like many in the world, they take it unkindly when they meet a Brit, American or Australian who seems to be taking unfair advantage.

Incidentally, not everybody sees it as an advantage. An Italian businessman says:

I feel sorry for the expatriot American manager: he can never be truly international. Let me give you an example. If I go to, say, Denmark, then what language do I choose?…English, of course. Just as it is when the American manager goes. The crucial difference is, when I go there, I have to stop being Italian…

6. Providing Insight

Some creators of artificial languages had aspirations to clarifying human thought. A logical language would make people think more logically. Mathematics is the only "language" that can show results in this direction. Unfortunately, mathematics will not help you get a drink at a crowded bar.

Learning a "real" foreign language is a way of gaining insight, and broadening your perspectives. The dominance of overseas English means that many native speakers of standard English do not bother. That is their loss.

I'm concerned, frankly, about this 1992 business. In language terms. They've all got a *natural advantage* over us, haven't they?

I mean, they all speak English already. How many of us speak German or Spanish or whatever? It hardly seems right somehow.

> English businessman (author's
> italics)

Message for native speakers of English

Murphy's Law, as it applies to language in international business, states: "When you have spent five hundred hours of your precious time learning the rudiments of business French, then and only then will the board post you to Dusseldorf."

You would do better to spend a little time learning to speak overseas English. It is a more useful instrument than school French, school German, or the English you speak at home.

Why English Hurts

Every language has its own special tortures for the learner. Slovene has not only singular and plural, but also a special set of *dual* forms. In Hungarian, to say "in" Budapest, Eger or any other Hungarian town requires different grammatical forms from those needed to say "in" Detroit, Bogota, or any town anywhere else. Koreans places their listener in one of six social gradings when they choose a verb suffix.

This section consists of seven sketches of various painful aspects of standard English that might not have occurred to you if you are a native speaker. We hope to encourage you to be more sympathetic to those who have learnt it from zero, to be more tolerant of their mistakes, and perhaps to modify your own way of talking.

1. Time

Every student of English-as-a-foreign-language will agree: the correct use of verb tenses is one of the biggest headaches. No other language makes quite the same distinctions between "He smokes" and "He's smoking", between "I smoked for years" and "I've been smoking for years". There are several extra colors in the English rainbow, it seems, when verbs and time meet.

But verbs are not the only tricky area. The distinction between "by next Friday" and "until next Friday" is elusive, as is the exact difference between "finally" and "at last". "Already", "yet", "just", "still", "always", "again", "before", "ago"—all are much more difficult to handle than "cup and saucer" or "joint venture". Unconscious slips are frequent.

The wise user of overseas English always double-checks when time is an issue: "Can we just verify all dates and deadlines?..."

2. Parts of Speech

Newspaper headlines in English often confuse foreigners, even when the topic is well known to them. One reason lies in a trick peculiar to English: the self-same word can often be an adjective or a noun.

So "bus" is definitely a noun, until we use it in the phrase "bus driver", when it serves as an adjective. Consider the headline "Chicago bus driver pension plan dispute announcement."

Confusion can arise between "price list" and "list price".

Conversely, a word first met as a verb—I sleep, we copy, they read—can also appear as a noun—refreshing sleep, illegible copy, a good read.

3. Prepositions and Other Little Words

Prepositions are a gamble in many languages. When the dictionary tells you that *na* in Russian means "on", that doesn't mean you are right to say *na* Friday, or *na* target.

English often presents a difficult choice, using two different words where one serves both purposes in the overseas English user's home language. In German, *seit* covers "for 57 years" and "since 1934".

4. Contractions

The conversational habit of contracting "I am going" into "I'm going" can be tiring for the listener, but it is generally understood.

There is one notable danger: the contraction of "cannot" into "can't" (especially with a short New York "a"). A sentence like "I can't tell you the result before Friday" is easily misheard as "I can tell you..."

5. Register

Simply put, choosing the right "register" in a language means select-
ing the appropriate expressions and tone of voice for a given situation—and more particularly for the person to whom you are talking.
So there is one way of asking your teenage son to pass the salt and quite
another for the First Lady.

Modern English uses the word "you" for both the polite form of
address and the familiar ("thou" died some time ago). Native speakers compensate by using "could you possibly" or "perhaps you might"
when they are on their best behavior. When they choose the impera-
tive ("Close the door behind you!"), they use subtle inflections of
voice to avoid sounding like a sergeant major. Such nuances are not
easy for an outsider to master.

A Portuguese person speaking to a Greek in overseas English will
save time and effort by simplifying his register. The Greek is not likely to take offence, so long as there's a smile. Native speakers sometimes
take offence unnecessarily.

6. Connectors

In conversation, native speakers usually restrict themselves to a short
list of simple connectors: "We were hoping to launch the product in
April, but there was a transport strike, so we missed the launch date by
a month."

Overseas English speakers often favor more literary or legalistic
methods of coupling up their ideas: "however" and "therefore" are
stronger and clearer than "but", and "so". "Moreover", "nevertheless", "consequently", "as follows" and "with regard to" do not feel
pompous in spoken overseas English.

7. Obligation

There are quite subtle shades of meaning between "You mustn't
drink and drive" and "You don't have to do military service"—not to
mention "You don't have to be an expert to see that this is a fake", or
"You really must visit us next time you're in Seattle".

TEST (for native speakers of English)

In the best tradition of school language primers, we offer native speakers of standard English a test:

Translate the following into overseas English, trying to retain as much as possible of the original message, while accepting some loss of flavor:

1. It can hardly have escaped your attention that our competitors have been getting a jump on us of late.

2. Short of taking him out and shooting him, I don't see how we'll ever be able to ditch him.

3. Far be it from me to stick my nose in, but are you quite sure you're tackling the issue the right way?

4. I wouldn't for a moment want you to think I'm uninterested in what I half-guess you're about to say, but could I get a word in edgeways before you get rolling?

5. You took your time! What kept you?

Answers

1. As you know, our competitors have had an advantage recently.

2. I think it'll be very difficult to remove him. Do you have a gun?

3. I know that you're more experienced than me in this field, but could I suggest that you look at the options again?

4. Can I say something before you begin?

5. At last! Where were you?

Overseas English users often stumble. Again, it is a good idea to double-check when listening, and use less elusive forms—"necessary" and "possible"—when speaking.

How to Use Overseas English

1. Grade Your Language

English is an idiomatic language. An idiom enriches a language, but also presents a barrier.

"It's no use crying over spilt milk" is a proverb, not an idiom. The use of proverbs in overseas English can be irritating, partly because they use local cultural references ("Penny wise, pound foolish"), and partly because they often contain problem words. So the use of "Too many cooks spoil the broth" leads to tedious explanations of "broth", which is a rare word known to very few outsiders; the alternative is to say "Too many cooks spoil the soup".

"We must grasp the bull by the horns" is a cliche now, but in its younger days it was a vigorous figure of speech, a metaphor. Metaphors are fine in overseas English—again provided they contain no mystifying words. The advanced student of overseas English is often tempted to make his or her language more colorful by learning a battery of metaphorical cliches, but there are dangers. "A finger in every pie" can easily slip and become "A finger in every tart". We promise this is a real example*.

The English idioms that cause learners most serious problems involve the use of a handful of verbs—*be, have, do, make, go, put, take* and, above all, *get*, together with a longer list of adverbs and prepositions—*up, down, in, around, after, by, for, with, from, to, at, across, over, under, out, along...*

After a hard day, the husband had been instructed by his concerned wife to sit down and relax for an hour with the evening news-

---

*Note for non-native speakers: "He has a finger in every pie" means "He is involved in every aspect of business"; a pie and a tart are very similar in the kitchen, but "tart" is also a colloquial term for "prostitute".

paper while she fixed dinner. He was feeling fidgety, and she caught him on the way to the kitchen:

"What are you up to?"
"I'm just going to wash the salad…"
"Are you up to it?"
"Of course I am."
"Well, it's up to you."

This is also a real example. It translates into overseas English as follows:

"What are you doing?" (in a suspicious tone of voice).
"I'm just going to wash the salad…"
"But you're tired. Are you sure?"
"Of course I am."
"Well, it's your decision."

So the native speaker of standard English, which is saturated with such expressions, must learn to edit them out of his or her speech in order to communicate smoothly with speakers of overseas English.

2. Use the Full Range of Tone and Tempo

"Well, that was certainly the longest report I've ever written."

English is a tonal language—much more so than many of its Continental neighbors. A large part of the message is encoded in the way an utterance is delivered, so the sentence above can have several distinct meanings, according to where you place the emphasis, where you pause, and where your voice rises and falls.

Any outsider who has studied English by enlightened methods, or who has had real exposure to living English, is conscious of this. Some manage to reproduce the sound patterns accurately, and to use this extra dimension when they communicate. Others—less musically inclined, perhaps—import the tone systems from their own language.

Whether or not he or she "sounds English", your overseas partner will be sensitive to a greater or lesser extent to tonal nuances. One significant difference between good and bad speakers of overseas English is this: the good ones use a wide range of tone and tempo to strengthen their messages, while the bad ones sound flat and monotonous.

A message for everybody

Place stress on the key words, and punch your message out. After all, there is something in the nature of English that lends itself to the rhythms of rock music. Lennon and McCartney's classic world hits were written and recorded in what might be considered a variety of overseas English—simple, direct language delivered with great effect.

Make greater use of significant pauses, giving your audience time to digest what you have just said, creating an appetite for what you are about to say.

Message for standard English native speakers

Use natural intonation and breath-grouping.

> If you *speak*...like *this*...and *put* a bitta *music*...into what you *say*...your *part*ner can *fol*low...much *bet*ter.

It is harder for your partner to understand the loud-flat-delivery-of-evenly-spaced-words-one-at-a-time.

When you want to make a point clearly, you will naturally tend to slow down. Try to achieve the effect...by chopping your sentence...into idea-groups..., pausing after each.

Your listeners have been trained, either formally or by experience, to understand the contractions of spoken English—"Now we're gonna decide who's responsible for the contract they've signed". You run a serious risk of sounding patronizing (the "watch my lips" syndrome) if you slow down too much, and say "Now we are going to decide who is responsible for the contract they have signed." So don't.

Message for overseas English speakers

Do not make the mistake of confusing speed with fluency. As you make progress in English, there is a temptation to demonstrate your skill by speaking more quickly. Resist it.

3. Accentuate the Positive

"It isn't that I'm suggesting you couldn't solve the problem, but…"

A native speaker can take this sort of construction in his or her stride—perhaps. Any other listener goes into mental spasm for a moment—are you saying I can solve the problem, or the opposite? What was that old rule I learned at school about two negatives making an affirmative? What are you going to say next, and will I be able to keep up?

These intricate sets of negatives, nested one inside the other like Russian dolls, are typical of standard English (the language of diplomacy) but are very damaging in overseas English. If you catch yourself uttering one—and the momentary panic in your partner's eyes should alert you—stop and say: "Sorry, that wasn't very clear…We all know you *could* solve the problem, but…"

"If we don't invest in this plant, we won't be able to meet demand next year."

Statements like this are bad salesmanship. They create depressing pictures in the listener's mind. People respond more willingly to promises than to threats. Try: "If we invest in this plant, we'll be in a good position to meet demand…"

"Not a bad effort. Not bad at all."

Standard English, especially the British version, depends on complex patterns of understatement, irony and nuance of tone. Such mannerisms are often misunderstood, and can cause disappointment or worse. If somebody performs well, say "Well done. Excellent."

4. Show Warmth; Show Willingness

Cultural embarrassment, and lack of language subtlety, can put a brake on friendliness. Sad to relate, acquaintance in international business often stops short at "How was your flight? Good, let's get down to business", or "Of course you know him. Big guy. Glasses. Works in Treasury in Minnesota."

Warm and lasting relationships will be at a premium in the business world of the future; people are tired of "Wham-Bam-Thank You, Ma'am". If you want to stand out in the crowd, as a person interested in people, make use of social time and small talk to go a little deeper— as we suggested back in Chapter 3. How?

- By asking questions, *listening* to the answers, and asking supplementary questions:

  "Are you from a big family? What does/did your father do?"

  "Are you a city or country person at heart? If you had your choice, where would you live?

  "Are you a good cook? Specialities? Secrets?"

- By letting out a little more about yourself, as a signal that your partners can talk freely about themselves.

- By remembering that nearly everybody's favorite subject of conversation, finally, is himself or herself.

In language terms, overseas English is sometimes a little curt:

"Are you in pharmaceuticals?"
"Yes."
"Who do you work for?"
"Hoechst."

Standard English uses echoing devices to create reciprocal warmth:

"Are you in pharmaceuticals?"
"Yes, I am."
"Really? Who do you work for?"
"For Hoechst."

The trick is to *give more than the minimum* and *mirror your partner's tone.*

In our own culture, we often rely on subtle indicators to display or detect enthusiasm—particularly tone of voice—and are afraid of seeming naive or ingenuous. Across language barriers, or in the neutral territory of overseas English, unspoken signals rarely work. State your good intentions overtly, and state them often:

"This will help both of us."

"I'd really like to hear more about that."

"We're very keen to reach agreement on this."

5. Use Questions to Good Effect

Sometimes there's no better way of making a point than by asking a question—is there? And who knows that better than the seasoned professional communicator—the politican, the lawyer, the advertising man?

The salesman in particular understands the power of the "Yes-sequence":

"Now you're a businessman, aren't you?"

"Yes."

"Can I assume you're always interested in ways of reducing your overheads?"

"Yes."

"Do you sometimes worry about the size of your telephone bill?"

"Yes."

"Will you buy this patent telephone bill reducer?"

"Yes."

The technique has value in every language. Most businesspeople, operating in their native languages, recognize that value.

Yet transactions in overseas English often get stuck in the rut of statement and counter-statement.

Message to overseas English speakers

There are two probable reasons why you do not use enough questions.

- The formation of questions in English is difficult.

- Your language habitually uses "statement forms" to ask questions: "You are Signor Rossi?"; "It's time to start the meeting?"

Try this: next time you are going to a meeting, think in advance of the two or three points you want to make. Write them down using ten words for each. Now translate each into a question: "Can anybody here see a real alternative?"; "What have we learned from last year's poor results?"; "How many of our big customers today were small customers five years ago?" Use those questions to make your points at the meeting. The habit will grow on you.

Message to standard English native speakers

The questioner is under pressure in many ways. English grammar is not as straightforward as you assume. Questions can cause headaches. There are the mysteries of auxiliaries and modals (do, have, will, would, etc.): "What do cannibals eat? Who do cannibals eat? What eats cannibals? Who eats cannibals?"

There are nested questions: "Don't you think we should stop wondering why we didn't do well last time, and start thinking about who can do what to make sure we do do well next time?"

When you ask a question of an overseas English speaker, make sure your question is simple enough to be answerable. Then check that the answer is an answer to the question you asked.

6. Keep It Short and Simple—Sometimes

When people are being trained to make presentations, they are often exhorted to "Keep It Short and Simple" (KISS).

If they are standard English speakers preparing for a standard English-speaking audience, KISS often means opting for Saxon vocabulary—"feed" rather than "nourish", "target" rather than "objective", "dream" rather than "fantasize". Hamlet's "To be or not to be?" works better than "I am confronted by an existential dilemma".

However, if your audience includes a contingent from a Romance language base, the advice should be different. Their ears and minds are conditioned to process longer, more Latinate words more easily. Everyday conversation in Italy, Spain and France is peppered with words that seem abstract or high-flown.

So "We didn't sell as many as we'd hoped, I'm afraid" gives a Venezuelan listener trouble. More Latin would be: "Unfortunately, our revenue was inferior to our predictions." This is ugly by any standards, and good overseas English strikes a compromise with something like "Unfortunately, we didn't reach our sales objective".

The other part of the KISS principle—one idea per sentence—holds true in any language. "Because it was her grandmother's birthday and in spite of the dangers of the forest, Little Red Riding Hood, who was a good little girl..." is poor stuff. And in case you think it only happens in badly told fairy stories, here is an anonymous example from an in-house sales document:

> "Whereas each of these considerations treated in isolation may appear to be of minor importance, they will when totalled together make a useful contribution to overall cost reduction."

Try chopping that one up into digestible pieces.

7. Use Big, Bold Signposts

We have more than once in the last three chapters, made the point that a clear framework or agenda is essential for effective communication across cultures. Your traveling companion will relax and enjoy the trip if he or she knows the length and direction of the journey, and how many halts there will be for refreshment and exercise.

Markets, placed along the way, offer reassurance. Between native speakers of the same language, they are often brief and subtle. Indeed, it is considered rather pedestrian to sign off each point formally ("And that is all I have to say regarding the second item") before moving on ("so it is clearly time to turn our attention to item number three").

Overseas English is not afraid to be pedestrian occasionally, especially if clarity and security are at stake. "So much for X, let's move on to Y"; "That covers production, so what about sales?"; "Turning from Japan to Korea..."; "I think we're ready now to change the subject..."—such deliberate and obvious "discourse markers" make for harmony and control.

Native speakers of any language cut corners or jump over gaps when they are in a hurry. Standard English typically omits relative pronouns and conjunctions, and this can be worrying to the overseas listener. "I told the salesman you sent the prices he quoted were too high" is a bit of a strain for somebody whose native language would always use several extra words in such a sentence: "I told the salesman *whom* you sent *that* the prices *which* he quoted were too high." Not surprisingly, overseas English tends to point up the grammatical relationships in each sentence.

8. Summarize Often

There is an old saying about public speaking: "Tell them what you're going to say; say it; tell them what you've said". Again, it sounds repetitive and unexciting. Professional comics don't do that, do they? And magicians pull rabbits out of hats without all that tedious explanation. If you are a comic or a magician, carry on. For the rest of us, it is a good idea to learn to walk before we try to run.

Everybody at the meeting will love you if, from time to time, you provide a neat summary of the action so far. To be the summarizer gives you power: you are effectively deciding what the meeting has achieved so far. Your summary should be unambiguous, fair and immediately comprehensible to all present. Otherwise it will be worse than useless and everybody will hate you.

Remember that your summary should be shorter than the material you are summarizing—unlike many we have heard.

9. Don't Worry about Body Language

Television programs, handbooks and training courses that touch on "personal communication" often dwell on body language, emphasizing areas of difference between cultures: Sicilian males embrace, while Swedish males do not; it is wrong to show the soles of your feet to an Arab; never touch the head of a Thai; and so on.

People are fascinated, because the messages are directed at a human weak spot—insecurity about how others perceive us. But the advice and the warnings can have a damaging effect. The "communicator" enters his or her next transaction nervous of making a mistake, and the proceedings become stiff and unnatural.

Charles Darwin, the earliest scientific investigator into non-verbal communication, came to the conclusion: "All the chief expressions exhibited by man are the same throughout the world." That was in 1872.

In today's business world, just as overseas English is penetrating everywhere, so there are standards in body language that are universally recognized.

- When you meet your partner *on neutral territory,* the universal code should be enough: smile, firm handshake, steady eye contact, relaxed but dignified bearing.

- *On your own territory,* point out any major gaffes to them ("In Japan, we show great respect to the business card..."), but otherwise be as flexible toward them as you would expect them to be with you.

- On their territory, find an opportunity to observe how people carry themselves and approach each other. Hotel lobbies are a good place. Then, if there is anything noticeably different, consider adapting your own style for the sake of harmony. But do nothing that might seem artificial or clumsy. Your overseas partner wants you to relax and be yourself.

Much of the communication between you will happen at a level deeper than words. Part of the purpose of meetings, of business travel, is to establish trusting relationships. How can your partner trust you if you are trying to be something you are not?

10. Add a Little Spice

Overseas English is not a language for writing great comedies or tragedies. Yet its most effective practitioners manage to be lively and stimulating.

Jokes, the rehearsed sort that begin "Have you heard the one about...?" should be used with care. The great majority depend for their humorous effect on some cultural or linguistic twist that does not travel well. If you find yourself in a joke-swapping session, the most workable are short, simple jokes about universal human foibles. The classic targets are avarice (the Scots, for example, have been very patient) and stupidity (an endless list of victims here—check the local scene). If you can avoid any suggestion of racism or sexism your listeners will be more comfortable. Self-deprecation, and the deprecation of your own culture, are welcome (and the best Jewish jokes are told by Jews).

That said, we are all in favor of *humor,* as is the overseas business community at large. Anecdotes often work better than set-piece jokes, especially if they are about the overseas world: "Do you know, I was checking out of a hotel in Djakarta a few weeks ago, and..."

When you have time to plan what you are going to say—a presentation, perhaps—you have the opportunity to design your message for maximum impact and memorability. Few of us are advertising copywriters, but most of us can rise to a little "colorful speech", and in the overseas world it counts for a lot.

Images and analogies are already present in large numbers in the basic business vocabulary: hands-on experience; turnkey projects; golden handshakes; and the product launch. All these are so familiar that the original image no longer comes to life in the mind of the listener; they are clichés. One fresh image within your presentation will work wonders: "Think of it as a..."; "This reminds me of that familiar moment when..."; "We've all had the experience, at one time or another, of...". As with humor, make sure the image you are suggesting "translates" into your listener's world. For example: in Western cultures, mice love cheese. In Eastern countries with no dairy tradition, they are more likely to be grain thieves. Talk of "bread-and-butter projects", "cash-cow products", and "creaming-off of profits" is also likely to confuse.

Rhyme and alliteration work perfectly well: "vision and decision"; "are we going to tell him the idea, or sell him the idea?"; "product, price and positioning." The non-native speaker enjoys grasping items of wordplay and passing them on to others.

The personal touch is also important. "Sales of the soft drink range climbed by 30 percent, owing to the high temperatures" has less appeal than "Another 30,000 hot, thirsty people were drinking Fizzipop".

Checklist for Both Overseas English and Standard English Speakers

If you try to improve in all ten areas at the same time, you will probably forget your own name.

So decide which *one* of the ten ideas could improve your performance in your next international meeting, re-read that section, and commit yourself to it.

"X" for commitment

1. Grade your language
   (I will take my partner's linguistic
   abilities into account)   _____

2. Use the full range of tone and tempo
   (I will put a little music and color into
   my speech)   _____

3. Accentuate the positive
   (I will be careful with irony and
   understatement)   _____

4. Show warmth; show willingness
   (I will be the first to break the ice, by
   word and gesture)   _____

5. Use questions to good effect
   (I will remember the persuasive power
   of questions, and use it)   _____

6. Keep it short and simple—sometimes
   (I will make my sentences short. I will
   put one idea in each)   _____

7. Use big, bold signposts
   (I will make sure my listener knows
   exactly where we are in the argument)   _____

8. Summarize often
   (I will pause and take stock regularly, for
   everybody's sake)   _____

9. Don't worry about body language
   (I will behave naturally and be myself)   _____

10. Add a little spice
    (I will find opportunities to bring my
    message to life)   _____

A Glossary of
Overseas English

The final section of this book is dedicated to more detailed observations on overseas English. We begin with an example of how communication can suffer when everyday words shift their meaning.

"Cross Purposes"—A Drama in One Act

Somewhere in Europe, Bob, a native speaker of English, is nearing the end of a meeting with Rene, a Continental European:

1 *Bob:*   How long are you here for, Rene?
2 *Rene:*   Since last night.
3 *Bob:*   No, I mean when do you have to leave for the airport?
4 *Rene:*   Oh. Twelve o'clock at the latest.
5 *Bob:*   Well in that case, we'd better press on.
6 *Rene:*   Sorry?
7 *Bob:*   Let's resume, shall we, or would you like some more coffee?
8 *Rene:*   No, let's resume. Would you like to?
9 *Bob:*   What?
10 *Rene:*   Resume.
11 *Bob:*   Yes, suits me. (A long silence, as Bob fiddles with his papers, and Rene gazes out of the window. Bob looks up.) Over to you, then.
12 *Rene:*   Ah! Yes! Well perhaps we could turn to the new quality control system. You say it's slowing things down...
13 *Bob:*   That's right. This week, for example, we're already two days late for one of my regular customers—half a dozen XB90s...
14 *Rene:*   Not an important order, then?
15 *Bob:*   I think it is!
16 *Rene:*   If you say so....What's your usual delivery delay on XB90s?
17 *Bob:*   No delay at all, if I can help it.
18 *Rene:*   But how much time do you need to turn an order round?
19 *Bob:*   We quote 14 days. It's all there in the report...
20 *Rene:*   And how long does it actually take?
21 *Bob:*   Fourteen days, of course! What sort of operation do you think I'm running? Look, I'm sure we can all see benefits coming from a really effective control system, but...

22 *Rene:*   I think it's early to talk about benefits, don't you?

23 *Bob:*   (Now quite exasperated) It was you who persuaded me 12 months ago to invest in the thing. Now you're casting doubt on the whole exercise. Terrific! Really terrific!

24 *Rene:*   I think that's an exaggeration, Bob. There's no real cause for alarm...

Can you feel Bob and Rene's frustration? If you want to work out what's going wrong, turn to the glossary on pages 154–62 and look up the words *since, resume, important, delay, actually, benefits* and *terrific*—the stumbling blocks which first appear in lines 2, 7, 14, 16, 20, 21 and 23 respectively of the dialogue above.

Standard English is a hybrid language; it has drawn on European originals at various times in its history. Down the centuries, certain standard words have developed strains different from their Continental cousins. Many of the terms treated in this glossary are close to their pre-English roots.

A German recognizes the word "meaning" as closely related to *Meinung* (opinion), and is naturally inclined to use it in similar ways; likewise the Italian who uses "sympathetic" as he uses its Italian cousin *simpatico* (nice). These hidden traps in the English language are so abundant that the French have a special term for them: *les faux amis* (false friends)—words that seem to mean the same but do not.

Japanese or Hungarian readers might be perplexed by some of the examples in this glossary, since their native languages are remote from standard English, and offer few opportunities for *interference* to take place. ("Interference" describes the involuntary transferring of a word or construction from one language to another.) However, they might find the glossary useful when they are perplexed by what a Colombian or an Austrian says to them in his or her version of English.

Many innovations in overseas English have occurred where interference from other languages is so frequent that it has produced an acceptable form—the "common practice" line so common in linguistic development.

This effect is likely in cases where the deviation from standard English carries no penalty. For example, "Telephone to me" is prescriptively "wrong", and teachers of English work hard to eradicate the "error" in their foreign students. Yet if the students are studying English in a practical rather than an academic spirit, they find it hard to care. The construction is clear and unambiguous, and causes no pain to other speakers, so why worry? (Similarly "I will pay my groceries"; "Can we meet us at 2:30?"; "How much did you buy that?" and many others.)

Overseas English often shrugs off distinctions in standard English that are hard to fathom and bring little benefit in terms of communication. Many European languages make no distinction between "make" and "do", "let" and "leave" or "like" and "as"—one word does the job perfectly well. The overseas practitioner tends to use the words interchangeably.

Sometimes it is not the *meaning* of the word which is at issue, but its *connotations* (e.g., the wartime associations of "collaborator"), or its force (e.g., "satisfactory", which carries far more positive feeling in overseas English than in standard English.

This glossary is aimed principally at native standard English speakers. It throws light on some of the confusions which lurk beneath the surface of overseas conversations, especially with European partners. It will also be useful to non-native speakers who want to be sure that their messages are both "correct" and clear.

Glossary

The glossary concentrates on individual words. The definition or explanation given first in each case relates to overseas English. The material in square brackets clarifies standard usage, but does not offer a full definition of the word: that is the job of a proper dictionary or an English teacher.

Where appropriate, we have indicated "language of origin" with the international symbols (D for Germany, E for Spain, etc). If there is no such indication, the usage is widespread.

We have subjective opinions about the items in this glossary. Some of them seem ugly, but are likely to survive and even supplant standard terms (e.g., "rentability"). Others are quite inoffensive to the English ear, yet they will probably remain "incorrect" (e.g., "formation").

Just as the world's business lingua franca has absorbed much of its vocabulary from American corporate English in the last few generations, so the resurgence of a united Europe could reverse the traffic a little: international meetings in Chicago might begin to accept a pan-European view on the real meaning of "eventually".

We do not claim that the list is comprehensive; we would be delighted to receive fresh examples for future editions.

D = Germany **E** = Spain **F** = France **I** = Italy **S** = Sweden

Abbreviations are often pronounced as words—so *f.o.b.* (free on board) is *fob.* Similarly *cif, vip, ira* and even *rip.* [All these are pronounced letter-by-letter in standard English.]

Achieve, *finish,* as in "We have achieved the project." [*Reach,* as in "We have achieved our objective."]

Actions, *shares,* as in "I sold my actions at just the right moment".

Actual, *current,* as in "our actual Personnel Director", [*Real,* as in "Our actual sales in 1989 were better than we expected."]

Actually, *at the moment,* as in "They are reviewing the situation actually." [*In fact,* as in "Actually, my name is Jane not Jean."]

Advices, *see* **Informations**

Agenda, *diary,* as in "Let me look in my agenda." **D** [The *order of business,* as in "How can we cover this agenda in two hours?"]

Agree, often "I am agree", or "I am agreed" in overseas English. A good example of a deep-rooted "error" which in no way disturbs communication.

All right, *see* **Satisfactory**

Anonymous, sometimes used to describe a company with anonymous shareholders, i.e., a public company. (From *société anonyme,* etc.)

Apparently, 1. *obviously,* as in "Would you like to improve productivity?"—"Apparently!" **F** 2. *Only apparently,* as in "Apparently he accepted my advice, but I don't think he was listening." **I** [*It seems,* or *People are saying,* as in "Apparently our competitors are in financial trouble".]

As, *see* **Like.**

Assist, *attend,* as in "Can you assist to the conference?" **F** [*Help,* as in "He assisted me at a difficult moment".]

At last, *lastly,* with no dramatic overtones, as in "And at last it is time to fix a date for the next meeting." **D** [In standard English, there is a sense of tension and relief, as in "At last you are here! We had almost lost hope."]

Benefit, *profit,* as in "a record benefit." **F** (*Advantage,* as in "The benefits can't be measured in financial terms".]

Charge, *load,* as in "I didn't know the gun [or the ship] was charged." (*Demand* a price, as in "This supplier is charging us too much".]

Collaborator, *colleague,* as in "I must give credit to all collaborators". [Connotation: *traitor,* as in "The collaborators were punished when the occupying army had retreated."]

Comfortable, *convenient,* as in "A 10:30 appointment is quite comfortable for me."

Compensate, *compensate for,* as in "Big sales at Christmas compensated the bad summer."

Competence, 1. *competition,* as in "We are facing serious competence". **E** 2. *Span of control,* as in the traditional, but often forgotten standard English usage "This project is outside my competence." **D, I**

Competent, *able,* or *well qualified,* as in "They tell me the anaesthetist is competent," **S** [This statement in standard English is not what you want to hear as they wheel you to the operating room. It means he is not completely useless, but not very good at his job.]

Concurrent, *competitor,* as in "We must watch our concurrents carefully", [*Simultaneous,* as in "The advertising campaign will run concurrently with the special price promotion".]

Conductor, *driver.* [Ticket collector or inspector, on public transport in most English-speaking cities.]

Conference, *lesson,* or *presentation,* as in "He made an excellent conference and nobody fell asleep". [A meeting for consultation or discussion.]

Control, *check,* as in "From time to time I control his expenses claims." [*Direct,* as in "I am not too old to control the department!"] So "quality control" in standard English gives a mental picture of continuous management of all factors affecting quality, while in overseas English it suggests a sampling procedure at some late stage of the production process.

Curiosity, *curious item or fact,* as in "I found several curiosities in the annual report." [In standard English this usage is obsolete. Dickens wrote "The Old Curiosity Shop" a long time ago.]

Daughter company, *subsidiary.* **D** With its companion "Mother company", it has a friendly feel which might displace the rather bald standard English terms. *See* **Holding.**

Definite, *final,* as in "She has definitely closed down the factory." [*Certain,* as in "We have no definite candidates yet".]

Delay, *lead time,* as in "How long is your usual delay on this product?" **F** [Lateness, as in "We apologize for the delay, which is partly due to a fire in our factory".]

Demand, *ask for,* as in "I offered them coffee or tea, and most of them demanded tea". **F** [Stronger in standard English, as in "The terrorists demanded the release of their comrades".]

Design, *draw,* as in "He designed his company organization chart on the back of a menu". **F** [*Create/engineer,* as in "He designs uniforms for airline staff."/"Who designed this equipment?"]

Dismiss, *resign,* as in "She had an argument with her boss and dismissed the company". **F** [*Fire,* as in "He dismissed me when I failed to reach my targets".]

Do, *see* **Make**

Economy, *finance,* as in "Lars Olsson, Chief Executive, Economy" **S** [Used in standard English either of "the Brazilian economy", or as in "We must cut costs; can you suggest any economies?"]

Employee, often suggests a higher position in the company than the standard English equivalent. This is more a matter of connotation than of definition. Experienced overseas English users know very well that ranks and grades and levels of power are difficult to express in one word, just as it is impossible to translate quickly and accurately from one legal system (or educational system) to another.

Engaged, *committed,* as in "We appreciate the engagement of your staff, who made us feel very welcome." **F** [*Hired,* as in "We engaged a new firm of auditors".]

Enjoy, often "I am enjoyed". (*see* **Agree**)

Equipments, *see* **Informations**

Eventually, *perhaps,* as in "We expect a return of 15, eventually 16, percent [*After a considerable time,* as in "Be patient; eventually this investment will give a good return".]

Excuse, *apology,* as in "I'm too busy to come to the meeting; please make excuses for me". **F** [*Justification* (often empty), as in "I don't accept your stupid excuses. You threw the ball; the ball broke the window".]

Exercise, *financial year,* as in "We expect a recession to start during this exercise." **F** [*Experimental project* or *maneuver,* as in "The whole exercise was a waste of time and money".]

Expect, *wait,* as in "I'll go and find somebody to help. You expect me here". **I**

Experience, *see* **Experiment**

Experiment, with **Experience,** one of a classic pair of false friends. **F** So overseas English speakers can produce: "Some of our most experimented researchers conducted the experience". [Standard English has the two ideas in reverse.]

Figures, *diagrams,* as in "The figures in this report tell us very little about the numbers involved". [*Numbers,* as in "I have a poor head for figures".]

For, sometimes *because,* as in "I cut the meeting short for I was in a hurry". **D** [This is rather an old-fashioned use of "for" in standard English.]

For, *by,* as in "our profits are up for 5 percent".

Formation, *training,* as in "We have cut the budget for formation". **F** [*Layout,* as in "an interesting geological formation".]

Funny, *enjoyable,* as in "The party at your house was rather funny". [*Amusing,* as in "He made a very funny after-dinner speech", or *strange,* as in "He has a funny attitude to women".]

Furnisher, *supplier,* as in "You are not the only furnisher of such services, you know…" **F** [*Supplier of furniture,* as in "Have you seen the office furnishers' catalogue anywhere? I need a new filing cabinet".]

Furnitures, *see* **Informations**

Get, a nightmare word in overseas English. Since it means everything and nothing in standard English, and there is always a more precise alternative, overseas English prefers "acquiring information" to "getting information". And in overseas English we "become old" while in standard English we "get old".

Great, *big,* as in "I don't like them, but they are a great company". **D** [*Excellent,* as in I'm staying in a great little hotel".]

Hardly, often *hard* or *forcefully,* as in "He presented his argument hardly". [In standard English, the idiomatic construction "I have hardly any money" means "I have almost no money". The adverb from "hard" is "hard".]

History, often *story,* as in "Have you heard the history about the traveling salesman…?" **F, I** [*Record of the past,* as in "The History of Ancient Rome".]

Holding, *holding company,* as in "Our holding is in Liechtenstein, but our operational headquarters is in Amsterdam".

Important, often simply *large,* as in "This is not an important investment, but it means life or death for the company". **F** [*Significant,* as in "Small details are very important in this job".]

In case, often *if,* as in "In case it rains, we will cancel the garden party". **F** [*As a precaution,* as in "We have hired a tent for the garden party in case it rains".]

Incoherent, often *inconsistent,* as in "You have made three incoherent statements". **F** [*Over-emotional and illogical,* as in "He was so angry his speech became incoherent".]

Informations, overseas English plural of "information", as in "He gave me three useful informations". Most languages have plurals also for "advice", "equipment", "furniture", "news", and so overseas English often uses them, too. [For a plural, standard English has "pieces of advice/equipment/etc".]

Interesting, *financially worthwhile,* as in "It's a standard project, but very interesting". **F** [*Fascinating,* as in "She lent me an interesting book".]

Investigate, often *invest,* as in "Have we investigated the money wisely?" **D** [Sherlock Holmes *investigates* crimes.]

Invite, often *treat,* as in "You paid for lunch yesterday. I invite you this time". **F** [Standard English has idioms like "This is on me", or "Let me *treat* you to lunch". "Invite" is mainly reserved for "They invited me home for the weekend," etc.]

Issue, *outcome,* as in "What was the issue of the meeting? I had to leave before the end." [*Discussion point,* as in "I'd rather not mention that issue in public".]

Leave, *see* **Let**

Lecture, *reading,* as in "He didn't understand the class when the professor was speaking, but he found the lecture easier". [*Lesson,* as in "I have to miss the nine o'clock lecture".]

Let, largely interchangeable with "leave", since most languages have one word here for both standard English meanings. So overseas English can produce "He let the lights switched on all night". [In standard English, "leave" is close to "forget"/"ignore", as in "Don't leave the decision to me!"; "let" is more like "permit", as in "Shall we let the secret out?"]

Like, largely interchangeable with "as", since most languages make do with one word for both sets of standard English meanings. So overseas English can produce "Really intelligent people, as my boss…" [In standard English, this example requires "like", as a near-synonym for "for example".]

Make, largely interchangeable with "do", since most languages use one word to cover what standard English sees as two distinct concepts. So OE can produce "They are making their homework." [In standard English, this example requires "doing", as a near-synonym for "performing".]

Many, *see* **Much**

Matter, used often in overseas English, as in "What do you think about that matter?" [Where standard English would be satisfied with "What do you think about that?"]

Mean, *believe. See* **Meaning**

Meaning, *opinion,* as in "We have different meanings". **D** Even in overseas English, this usage will probably not take hold.

Mother company, *parent company. See* **Daughter company. D**

Much, with "many", used in preference to "a lot of", as in "He made much money and many enemies". [In conversational standard English, "much" and "many" are common in the interrogative and the negative, as in "How much?" and "Not many". In the affirmative, "a lot of wine"/"a lot of bottles" is more frequent.]

Nearly, *approximately,* as in "One hundred and fifty Hungarian forints is worth nearly one U.S. dollar". [In standard English, *almost,* as in "The shock nearly killed me".]

Necessary, used in preference to tricky modals like "need" or "should". "Is it necessary to leave a tip?" might sound ponderous to native speakers, but it serves the purpose in overseas English, and is regular and easy to handle.

Newses, *see* **Informations**

OK, *excellent,* as in "Thank you very much. Your hospitality was OK". [Similar to "satisfactory" and "all right", which in standard English mean "tolerable".]

Other, often *different,* as in "His feelings are other". **D** [In standard English, "the other thing" might be exactly the same as "this thing"— separate, but not different.]

Obviously, *see* **Apparently**

Of course!, *certainly!,* as in "Are you ready for lunch?"—"Of course!" [*Naturally! Why do you ask?,* as in "Do you really believe in your product?"—"Of course!"]

One, often used, especially by Spanish speakers, as the unemphatic indefinite article in place of "a/an"—as in "they made one offer for the goods". [Standard English usually reserves "one" for emphasizing unity or singularity, as in "Give me one good reason to accept your offer."]

Particular, often *strange,* as in "Waiter, this fish tastes rather particular". **F** [overlap with standard English "peculiar"]

Partner, an increasingly popular term in overseas English, especially among Germans, to refer to anyone you have dealings with, suggestive of harmony and understanding. So "My supplier/client/banker/opposite number/agent" is becoming "my partner". Standard English has no good equivalent to this use of "partner", so we have adopted it in this book.

Peculiar, *see* **Particular**

Piece, *unit,* as in "The market for Easter eggs is enormous. We expect to sell half a million pieces this year".

Politics, often *policy,* as in "We have very strict politics on this matter". [In standard English, "politics" is either an academic subject or a dirty game.]

Possible, used in preference to tricky modals like "can" or "might": "Is it possible to use your phone?" might sound ponderous to native speakers, but it works fine in overseas English.

Possibly, *if possible,* as in "I'll fax you the information tomorrow, possibly". **I** (In standard English this sounds casual and uncaring—"maybe I will, maybe I won't".]

Pretend, *aspire,* as in "We are pretending to market the best-quality product". [*Simulate,* as in "He pretended to be asleep, but he was listening to every word".]

Prevision, *forecast,* as in "The market previsions for Hungary are optimistic". **F, I** [The word does not yet exist in standard English.]

Problem, often *item* or *issue,* with no gloomy connotations, as in "We have discussed this problem enough; we must move on to the areas of difficulty". [In standard English, "problem" always has unpleasant connotations, as in "Problems, problems, problems! Can't you think positive for a moment?"]

Profit, *see* **Benefit**

Protocol, often *minutes,* as in "I hope you all received the protocol of the last meeting". **D** [Correct procedure, as in "Does anybody know the protocol for dinner with an Irish Archbishop and a Saudi prince?"]

Quite, sometimes *absolutely* where it sounds like "fairly", as in "The results were quite good. Open the champagne…" [In standard English, "quite" means "totally" with absolute adjectives—"quite perfect" or "quite incredible". It only means "fairly" or "rather" with scalar adjectives—"quite heavy" or "quite well-written".]

Realize, *make real,* as in "They realized a big civil engineering project". [*Understand,* as in "I suddenly realized the scope of the problem".]

Red numbers, *the red,* as in "I'm afraid we're writing red numbers again". **D** [Standard English is more economical—"We're in the red".]

Remark, often *notice,* as in "I remarked that nobody else was formally dressed, but said nothing". [*Passed comment,* as in "She remarked to him that his prices were rather high".]

Resume, usually *sum up,* as in "The chairman resumed very succinctly". **F** [Recommence, as in "We'll resume after coffee". Resumé is also used as a noun to mean career history.]

Rentability, *profitability,* as in "a high-volume product with low rentability". **F** [The word does not yet exist in standard English.]

Responsible, *the responsible person,* as in "Could I speak to the responsible of management training, please?" Many adjectives in many European languages can be used without an accompanying noun—e.g., Hugo's *Les Miserables,* which translates rather uncomfortably into "The Miserable Ones".

Safe, often *secure,* as in "He wanted a safe job, so he became a policeman in New York". [In standard English, "safety" is usually a physical matter.]

Satisfactory, often carries stronger praise than in standard English, as in "Your contribution to the meeting was satisfactory". In overseas English, such a statement is cause for congratulations. The same goes for "Your samples seem to be all right". [In standard English, "satisfactory" and "all right" are used to describe things in a less positive way, as in "The food was all right, but I could have cooked it better myself."]

Say, *see* **Tell**

Sensible, often *sensitive,* as in "The market is very sensible to interest rates on loans". [*Reasonable/well-balanced,* as in "No fantasies, please; I want sensible suggestions".]

Shortly, *often briefly,* as in "please tell us the basic facts shortly". **D** [*Soon,* as in "Lunch will be served shortly".]

Since, often *for,* as in "I have known him since several years".

Society, often *company,* as in "before I joined my present society." **F, I** [Organization with voluntary members, e.g., Society for the Prevention of Cruelty to Animals]

Spare, *save,* as in "We can spare a little money by making it in plastic". **D** [*Give something from reserves,* e.g., "Can you spare some money for this charity?"]

Summary, sometimes *contents list.* **F**

Speak, *see* **Tell**

Sympathetic, *pleasant,* or *easy to get on with,* as in "He never offers to pay for lunch; I don't find him sympathetic". [*Kind to people in trouble,* as in "Thank you for listening so sympathetically to my problems".]

Talk, *see* **Tell**

Technique, often *technology,* as in "Bengt specializes in data transmission technique". **S** [*Skill* or *method,* as in "She always beats me at tennis; she has a very good backhand technique".]

Tell, with "say", "speak" and "talk", forms a group whose shades of meaning are often lost in overseas English. So "Tell me..." can easily become "Say me..." and so on. **I**

Terrific, often *frightening,* as in "I don't like terrific movies". **F** [Usually *very good,* as in "This sushi is terrific".]

Therefore, *that's why,* as in "We need a specialist for this job. Therefore I sent for you". **D** [In SE, "therefore" is used to introduce an idea which is new to the listener, as in "The offer is a fair one. We therefore recommend that you accept it".]

Until, sometimes *by,* as in "I promise to let you have the figures until lunchtime tomorrow". **D.**

Used to, a minefield. To give just one example: "I use to spend my weekends gardening" probably means in standard English "I usually spend…"

Vivacious, *hard-wearing,* as in "Our tractor tires are very vivacious". **F** [*Full of life* or—in Hollywood—*sexy,* as in "a vivacious blonde starlet".]

When, often *if,* as in "When you agree with me…" **D** [The standard English distinction here is also an important one in many other languages, and will probably survive in "correct" overseas English.]

With pleasure!, *Yes, please!* **F**

Word, give the, *hand over to,* as in "That's all from me. I'll give the word to Dr. Mueller".

Wrong, you are, *I'm afraid I can't agree.*

Yes, covers a range of meanings from "You are absolutely right and I agree to do as you suggest" to "I am listening to what you are saying but reserving judgment until I work out what you really mean". For cultural rather than linguistic reasons, this latter meaning is especially common among the Japanese. We can only suggest you check from time to time.

Further Reading

1. Culture

The Economist Business Traveller's Guides, Economist Publications.
Series of guide-books including cultural and economic background, available for a dozen or more countries.

Edward T. Hall (1959) *The Silent Language,* Doubleday.
Introduction to the effects of cultural differences on everyday life.

Henry Hobhouse (1985) *Seeds of Change,* Sidgwick & Jackson.
Economic history of sugar, tea, cotton, quinine, potato, illustrating development of cultures.

Gerd Hofstede (1980) *Culture's Consequences,* Sage.
Detailed statistical survey of cultural attitudes in business.

John Hutton (1988) *The World of the International Manager,* Philip Allen.
Provides good summary of Hofstede's findings, pp 121–7.

Michael Porter (1990) *The Competitive Advantage of Nations,* Macmillan.
Substantial research on causes of economic rise and fall of nations.

2. Company

James Dudley (1989) 1992—*Strategies for the Single Market,* Kogan Page.
Survival strategy and opportunities in the European Single Market.

Michael Goold and Andrew Campbell (1987) *Strategies and Styles,* Basil Blackwell.
Examines the role of the corporate center in managing diversified corporations.

Charles Handy (1989) *The Age of Unreason,* Business Books.
How changes in demographics will affect careers and business structures.

John Harvey Jones (1988) *Making it Happen,* Collins.
Distillation of his experience as chairman of ICI.

Robert Townsend (1984) *Further Up the Organization,* Michael Joseph.
Former CEO of Avis continues lighthearted assault on formal business structures.

3. Character

R. Meredith Belbin (1981) *Management Teams,* Heinemann.
Analysis of eight types of team members and how best to combine them.

Tony Buzan (1974) *Use Your Head,* BBC.
Tips on how to learn and how to communicate.

D. Mackenzie Davey (1989) *How to Be a Good Judge of Character,* Kogan Page.
Accessible introduction to business applications of psychology.

Genie Laborde (1983) *Influencing with Integrity,* Syntony.
Neuro Linguistic Programming and Business communication.

Peter Russell (1979) *The Brain Book,* Routledge Kegan Paul.
Covers similar ground to Buzan, with more of the scientific background.

4. Tactics

John A. Carlisle and Robert C. Parker (1989) *Beyond Negotiation,* John Wiley & Sons.
Makes the link between corporate culture and negotiation style. A "green" approach.

Roger Fisher and William Ury (1982) *Getting to Yes,* Hutchinson.
Now a standard, the Harvard Negotiation Project's text on collaborative negotiation.

Roger Fisher and Scott Brown (1989) *Getting Together,* Hutchinson.
On building relationships.

Antony Jay (1971) *Effective Presentation,* British Institute of Management.
A thoughtful yet practical handbook.

Gavin Kennedy (1984) *Negotiate Anywhere,* Business Books.
Tactics for various target countries.

John Mole (1990) *Mind Your Manners,* The Industrial Society.
Comparison of business styles and approaches in the EC Twelve.

5. Timing

Jeremy Campbell (1989) *Winston Churchill's Afternoon Nap,* Paladin.
Timekeepers in the human body.

Paul Watzlawick (1976) *How Real Is Real?* Random House.
Popularized science: time perception, communication and much more.

G. J. Whitrow (1988) *Time in History,* Oxford University Press.
Mechanics of measurement and attitudes to time throughout history and in various cultures.

Michael Young (1988) *The Metronomic Society,* Thames & Hudson.
Rhythms of nature and agriculture compared to modern timetabling.

6. Talk

Bill Bryson (1990) *The Mother Tongue,* Hamilton.
Light history of the English language.

David Crystal, ed. (1987) *Cambridge Encyclopedia of Language.* Cambridge University Press.
Readable coverage of many areas of language.

Edward T. Hall (1966) *The Hidden Dimension,* Doubleday Anchor.
Cross-cultural survey of personal space.

Desmond Morris (1977) *Manwatching,* Jonathan Cape.
Popular account of nonverbal behavior, including some cross-cultural comparisons.

Gerard I. Nierenberg and Henry H. Calero (1973) *How to Read a Person Like a Book,* Hanau.
Body language, mainly from U.S. perspective.

The Authors

Vincent Guy and **John Mattock** are management consultants and trainers, specializing in international business communication.

Since 1975, they have been working with executives from leading organizations in Europe, the United States and Japan.

The authors have run programs on international culture at Canning International Management Development, a training center operating in London, Bath, Milan and Tokyo, and employing 80 consultants worldwide.

In 25 years, Canning has helped 40,000 managers from dozens of countries to improve their performance as communicators.

Index

TITLES OF INTEREST IN
BUSINESS AND BUSINESS TRAVEL

For further information or a current catalog, write:
NTC Business Books
a division of NTC Publishing Group
4255 West Touhy Avenue
Lincolnwood, Illinois 60646-1975 U.S.A.